Scaredy Cat

© Bob Bonn 1997

Baja Magic

LEGEND

1 - Tijuana
2 - Ensenada
3 - La Bufadora
4 - Scammon's Lagoon / Guerrero Negro
5 - Malarrimo Beach
6 - San Ignacio Lagoon
7 - San Ignacio
8 - Todos Santos
9 - Cabo San Lucas
10 - San Jose Cabo
11- Santiago
12- Buena Vista
13- Los Barriles
14- La Paz
15- Loreto
16- Bahía Concepción
17- Mulege
18- Santa Rosalía
19- Bay of Los Angeles
20- Gonzaga Bay
21- Cataviña
22- San Felipe
23- Mexicali
24- Tecate

Map Illustration & Design by Glen Malecki

Cactus Cat

© Bob Bonn 1997

Cooking with Baja Magic

Mouth-Watering Meals From The
Enchanted Kitchens and
Campfires of Baja

By Ann Hazard

To Greg—
It's been a blast!
Enjoy y
¡Buen Provecho!

¡Olé! ♡
Ann
Hazard

Cooking With Baja Magic is dedicated
to my parents, Dottie and Togo Hazard
who took me and my sister, Nina, all over Baja
as children---forever reminding us
to lock the memories
up tight in our hearts---
where we would never lose them.

———————————————

A portion of the profits will be donated to various Baja charities.

Author: Ann Hazard
Editor: Nina Hazard Baldwin
Illustrator: Bob Bonn
Book Design: Terri Zumstein
Cooking With Baja Magic
First Edition First Printing November, 1997

Printed in the United States of America

Library of Congress Catalogue Card Number:
Hazard, Ann L.
Cooking With Baja Magic
ISBN 0-9653223-1-9

I. Cookbook
II. Travel

———————————————

Acknowledgments

Obviously, my gratitude is first and foremost to my family. Without my parents Dottie and Togo Hazard, none of this would have ever happened. I want to thank my sister, Nina Hazard Baldwin, (President of Renegade Enterprises) whose intelligence and incomparable business sense is enhanced by a lively sense of humor and passion for living life to its fullest. I want to thank my children, Gayle and Derek Tresize who are patient and reasonably quiet when I'm writing, and who are so proud of the fact that they're "Fourth Generation Baja Rats." I thank my Uncle George and Aunt Hope up in heaven for all the awesome times we had camping when I was a kid. And of course, I'm grateful to my grandfather, Pappy Hazard, a real honest-to-God cowboy from the Wild West who, along with his buddies Erle Stanley Gardner and Francisco Muñoz, practically invented Baja Magic.

I'm deeply indebted to Bob Bonn, who has added his whimsical, delightful art to this book. I thank Mary and John Bragg of Restaurant Pancho's in Cabo San Lucas, Marc Spahr of Caffé Todos Santos, the wonderful people at the Palapa Azul and the La Concha Beach Resort in La Paz who shared their favorite recipes with us, not to mention Tío Pablo's in Los Barriles, Chuy Valdez and crew at The Buena Vista Beach Resort, Punta Morro in Ensenada, the La Bufadora foursome: Celia's, Gordos, The El Dorado and Restaurant La Bufadora. And of course, I have to mention the waiters and chefs (from places like Hotel Caesar's in Tijuana, and the El Presidente Hotel in Mexico City) who have shared their secret recipes with my mother in years past — thank you too!

I'm grateful to Terri Zumstein for her wonderful sense of design and color. She definitely caught the spirit of Baja Magic as she put this book together. I thank my friends too, who have believed in and encouraged me over the years to finally get this book into print: Kathy Alward, John Baldwin, Lily Doris, Jerry Snow, Sue and Jim Graham, Kit, Doris and Netter Worthington, the Chadwell family, Antonio Cristerna, Kim Ryan, Susan Monken, Leslie Eady, Susanne Swenddal, Nancy and Jim Peevey, Gene Kira, Ginger and Chuck Potter, Christy and Chuck Geiling, Heidi Osborne, Heather Borer, the León family (our La Bufadora patrons), all our great La Bufadora neighbors, my buddies at Discover Baja, Susan Hill and all my other cousins, aunts and uncles. And last but not least, another big thanks to someone in heaven: Jack Smith, a phenomenal writer and ongoing source of inspiration to me.

TABLE OF CONTENTS

TABLE OF CONTENTS

TABLE OF CONTENTS

JUST WHAT IS BAJA MAGIC?

Tres Amigos

Travel as far south and west as you can in this country without leaving the mainland and you end up in San Diego. Head further south, cross the world's busiest border and you're in Tijuana — Baja California — Mexico.

My sister, Nina and I grew up on this bi-cultural piece of real estate. So did my dad, and his father before him. My grandpappy raised cattle on ranches spanning both sides of the dotted line, back in the early part of this century when there was no line, when immigration wasn't legal or illegal and the only thing that divided our two countries was a lonely outpost on a dirt road going — as Jimmy Buffett would say — south.

When I was a child, Baja was Never-never Land, a place where I felt more at home than in my own hometown. It was a place of endless empty hills, sunny skies and see-through aquamarine water teeming with fish. A smiling, brightly colored place of leather-skinned cowboys who tossed us high into the air, sang Mariachi ballads and danced to songs like La Bamba. Nina and I ate tacos before we ate hot dogs. We ate them every day for breakfast on our first trip to La Paz, back in 1962. We learned to speak Spanish before kindergarten. And we loved it all. Still do.

Why? Well, let me tell you a couple of secrets about Mexicans. They believe life is to be enjoyed, that integrity is paramount and that God and family are more important than money. They may live in a third world country, but guess what? They don't think they're deprived. They think we're ridiculous with our obsession to hoard and discard possessions. Raise the hood of any ancient (but roadworthy) Baja troque (truck) and you will instantly appreciate Mexican ingenuity. These folks are more resourceful than you could ever imagine. They've raised recycling to an art form. And — they will use even the lamest of excuses to throw a fiesta. From gray-haired grannies to Pampers-clad toddlers, everyone gets into the spirit of revelry. Food abounds, cerveza (beer) and tequila flow and music blares. Do they count fat grams? Hardly. They consider it just another example of our gringo (that's us, we're the gringos) lunacy.

Back in the mid-fifties when my parents first took me and my sister to Baja, most of their friends thought they were nuts. We were sure to be robbed by banditos, they said. If not, we'd ingest toxic amoebas and come down with Montezuma's Revenge. But my dad has some serious cowboy blood in him, and even though my mom swears she never stepped off Wilshire Boulevard (90210) until she graduated from high school, she's part renegade too. (She just doesn't like to admit it.) We spent our vacations traveling in Baja and mainland Mexico every year when I was growing up —and nothing bad ever happened to us. We visited cities and seaside resorts; we took our camper to remote beach and mountain villages where we were the only gringos for miles.

My mother let me loose in the kitchen early on. We became partners in culinary crime, plagiarizing together as we recreated our favorite meals from trips south of the border. Over the years we collected recipes and kept them in a file box I made myself. Later on I spent time in Spain, the Imperial Valley of California, Colorado and New Mexico. Each time it was back to the kitchen. More trial and error. My file box eventually outgrew itself and I typed up my first cookbook in 1981. This was a good move on my part, because I was tired of being the designated chef whenever a fiesta was called for. Soon my friends were inviting me over for dinner. (Yes!)

You know, I still go south every chance I get. My family now has a second home in La Bufadora, a few miles south of Ensenada, at the tail end of what the L.A. Times has labeled, "Baja's Romantic Gold Coast." Our electricity is solar there. Our refrigerators run on propane. Our phones (if we have them) are cellular. There's no mail. Our water is hauled in by truck and stored in pilas, which are concrete water tanks. (No, we don't drink pila water.) If we want to visit neighbors, we spy on them first with our binoculars. (Yes, you could say we are a community of voyeurs.) If we get a positive sighting, we strap on our hiking sandals and cruise on over.

La Buf (pronounced Boof), as we call it, is a gringo colony on a private ranch owned by Señor José León Toscano, our patrón. Like every other gringo colony in Baja, it is, to its expatriate residents, an antidote to late twentieth century civilization — a place where everyone knows our names and an outback where kids can run free. And like most other accessible places in Baja, it's changing — it's growing and it's becoming more Americanized. To me, La Buf epitomizes Baja Magic. Why? Because Baja is raw and remote, set apart and somehow untouched by the chaos and despair of our world. It draws people unto itself like a magnet and it is against the backdrop of its mountains, deserts and endless beaches that we Baja Rats reconnect with the essence of who we are. I, like everyone else whose soul has been captured and forever held prisoner by Baja's unique magic, am humbled by the vastness of its emptiness, the wildness of its waves in winter, the profusion of its stars at night and the magnificence of the ever-present pods of grey whales that cruise up and down its coastline from early winter through spring.

Cooking With Baja Magic is the story of my life and travels. If you're still wondering what Baja Magic is, let me clarify something. Baja Magic isn't a style of cooking or a new type of cuisine — it's an attitude. To cultivate it is to focus on the beauty in God's creations — not our own. To cultivate it is to kick off your shoes, put on some festive Latin music and heave a huge sigh that casts off the cares of our crazy, mixed-up world. To cultivate it is to imagine yourself in a simpler, gentler place, celebrating life and beauty with people you love. Baja magic is about savoring life. It's about sharing. Caring. Laughing. It's about accepting that life is full of question marks and richly infused with mystery and paradox — and it's about not minding that we don't have all the answers.

Jack Smith mirrors my feelings about Baja in his book, **God and Mr. Gomez:**[1]
" ... I felt a pleasant weightlessness, as if the Baja Peninsula had been detached from the continent at the border and was drifting away in this blue sky and silver sea, just as the Spaniards had imagined. My burdens had been left behind on the mainland, and were receding out of sight, out of mind."

This cookbook has one purpose — to tip your perspective slightly to the south by injecting you with some Baja Magic. So, hey — come on! Dare to throw a fiesta! It can be a dinner for two, a party, a backyard barbecue or a meal for your family. Just kick off those shoes, crank up the mariachi tunes and start dancing while you cook!

Ole!

1 Smith, Jack, **God and Mr. Gomez**, New York: Reader's Digest Press, 1974

SALSAS

Mi Casa es Su Casa

In the beginning there were chiles. More than 40 different kinds that I know of. Then there was salsa. More varieties of salsa than you could ever imagine.

No Baja meal is complete without salsa. You know it — it's a spicy sauce made from fresh or canned chiles, tomatoes, onions and spices that's eaten with chips or spooned over food to liven it up. It can be mild or it can be so hot it'll blow your head off. When you visit a Mexican restaurant, you're probably served a bowl of it to scoop up with tortilla chips while you're waiting to order.

In the recipes that follow, I use several varieties of chiles. Fresh chiles can be found in markets all over the Southwest, and of course anywhere in Baja. However, in other parts of the U.S. it may be necessary to go to a Latin American market to locate some of the more exotic types. I don't use exotic chiles very often — too much hassle. But when I do, I offer substitutions or suggest canned chiles to keep you from going crazy if you don't live in an area with a large Hispanic population. I've also specified brands of prepared salsas that I like, for those times when you just don't have the time or inclination to make your own salsas.

Rest assured, I'll tell you know how hot a salsa is before you make it. I won't pull a fast one on you that will ruin your reputation as a culinary magician for life as your guests scream out the front door, heading for Baskin-Robbins to chill out their palates. I promise. And I've spared you the infamous habanero chile, that notorious "chile from hell." However, if you're curious, you can find habanero salsa if you look hard enough and try it out. I did. I like it. But then I have — I confess — a cast iron palate. And fresh habanero chiles are still too hot for me! In fact, on the chile scale they are rated number 40. For comparison purposes, Jalapeños come in at number four; serranos at number six. And, unlike a leather-mouthed friend of mine named Sue, who won the Chile Eating Contest at the Hussong's Chili Cook Off in Ensenada two years in a row (23 serranos in 3 minutes), I cannot eat a single serrano without a certain amount of distress!

Another key ingredient in salsas and many other regional border dishes is cilantro. Cilantro is otherwise known as "Chinese parsley" or "coriander" and can be found fresh in most parts of the west. It's also available dried, or you can grow your own from coriander seeds, which are found in the spice section of any supermarket.

Go for it! You may become a salsaholic like me and my sister, Nina. She claims that salsa raises the metabolism and releases endorphins, thus burning fat while enhancing the diner's sense of well-being. Hey! Sounds feasible to me and a whole lot more fun than sweating one's tail off at the gym!

SALSA FRESCA

My lineage is solidly comprised of cow-boys (on my dad's side) and artists (on my mom's). My dad's family found its niche in the twentieth century in the construction business. Every Christmas for 40 years I was invited to a construction company barbecue at my dad's office. In true Baja fashion, the meat was cooked over grills fashioned from split oil drums and served with home-made tortillas, salsa, beans and guacamole. The chef's name was Carlos and every other day of the year he worked as a laborer, cleaning up jobsites.

He recited this recipe to me several years ago in Spanish during a Christmas party. The ingredients may be varied, depending on how hot you like your salsa. If you're unsure, experiment. If your salsa turns out too spicy, add more tomatoes. If it's too mild, add more jalapeños or yellow guero chiles.

Aside from being served as an accompaniment to nearly every dish in this cookbook, salsa can also be served as an appetizer with chips. If you don't have time to make your own salsa, Herdez Salsa Casera (Mexican red sauce) or Embasa Salsa Casera are good substitutes. I also keep Pico Pica Hot Sauce and Durkee Red Hot Cayenne Pepper Sauce on hand at all times because their flavors are unique. When in Baja, Salsa Huichol or Salsa Amor are my preferences. In-A-Pinch Campsite Salsa (recipe immediately following) can be substituted for salsa fresca when fresh ingredients are unavailable.

5 - 10 fresh jalapeño (small, green, very hot) chiles
5 - 10 fresh guero (small, yellow, very hot) chiles
2 - 5 fresh Anaheim chiles (long, green, mild)
10 - 12 medium-sized tomatoes
2 onions
4 garlic cloves
1 large bunch cilantro
1 1/2 tbsp beef bouillon powder
1 tsp lemon juice

Wash all chiles and tomatoes and remove stems. In a large Dutch oven, place chiles and tomatoes in about one inch water. Bring to boil and simmer for two to three minutes.

Remove from stove and cool for a few minutes. When you can handle the chile mixture, drain off about half the water and mince, by hand or in the food processor. Put all minced chiles and tomatoes in a large bowl. Dice onions and garlic in food processor and stir into chile mixture. Wash cilantro and cut off the longest portion of the stems. Dice remaining part of the plant in the food processor. Stir into salsa.

Add lemon juice and bouillon. Stir well. Place in quart size jars and refrigerate. Depending on quantities of chiles and tomatoes you use, this should make two to three jars of salsa. It's best if refrigerated at least eight to twelve hours and will keep for several days in the refrigerator.

IN-A-PINCH CAMPSITE SALSA

Aside from being San Diego pioneers and builders, my Grandfather, Pappy and his sons, Bruce and Togo were some of the first Baja Rats. My dad (Togo) loves to tell the story of his first big fishing trip south. It was 1932 and he was ten years old. It took the trio over seven hours to traverse the 75 mile dirt road from Tijuana to Ensenada in their beat-up old Ford. Pappy's fish camp, which consisted of a tiny, completely primitive hut with an

attached outhouse, was located at Punta Banda — another two hours away, at the southern mouth of Todos Santos Bay. The road there was accessible only at low tide, so on many of their trips over the years, they had to wait half a day for the tide to recede. No matter. They always hung out with the locals and the hours sped by.

This salsa is made for times like those, when the nearest store is too far away to even contemplate. Keep the ingredients on hand, like I do and you can always make it in a pinch — whether you're in a remote part of Baja or at home and craving something Mexican. My mom always kept a store of these goodies in our camper, so that on our Baja trips, we could make salsa whenever the urge hit us. The recipe calls for canned tomatoes and canned chiles, which means that it's as quick as it is easy. It's also tasty and can be used in place of Salsa Fresca anytime.

1 1 pound, 12 ounce can Italian tomatoes, drained
1 onion
3 cloves garlic
2 - 8 canned jalapeños
1 tsp dried oregano

1 tsp dried cilantro (if not available, use oregano)
1 tbsp beef bouillon powder
2 tbsp American chili powder (mild)
2 tbsp lemon juice

Coarsely chop all ingredients, one at a time. Mix together in bowl. Place the salsa in a large saucepan and simmer for about twenty minutes. This makes approximately three cups and will keep for about ten days in the refrigerator.

SALSA RANCHERA — PANCHO VILLA STYLE

Rumor has it that Salsa Ranchera was invented by the vaqueros, or Mexican cowboys. After a hard day working the range, they would gather around the campfire, whip up a batch and spoon it over about anything. I believe that! Salsa Ranchera is wonderful over fried eggs (look for the recipe for Huevos Rancheros in the Breakfast & Brunch section). You can also pour it over omelettes, grilled chicken or turkey breasts.

At Pancho's Restaurant in Cabo San Lucas, where this particular recipe originates, owners Mary and John Bragg (by all means — check out "The Truth About Tequila" in the From the Bar section of this book for the scoop on John) serve it over their Chile Rellenos and use it as a key ingredient in their Pancho's Tortilla Soup. Read about Mary there, in the Soup section. And trust me, the mild, light and very tomato-ey taste of this salsa appeals to even the most sensitive palates.

4 whole green peppers, thinly sliced
8 large, ripe tomatoes, thinly sliced
2 large, white onions, thinly sliced
2 tbsp dried or fresh oregano,
6 bay leaves
6 tbsp powdered chicken bouillon (they use Knorr Suiza in Cabo)
4 tbsp olive oil
fresh ground black pepper to taste
salt to taste

Place peppers, onions and tomatoes in large skillet with the oil and saute until cooked. Add the seasonings and bouillon and cook about a half hour. Adjust seasonings and set aside. This recipe makes enough for twelve servings of tortilla soup, huevos rancheros, chile rellenos, etc. Mary recommends that you use half and store the other half in your freezer for the next time ....

SALSA VERDE

This green salsa is tangy and relatively mild. I know it may sound kind of weird to you if you're new to salsas, but you have to believe me when I tell you that it's really, really good. In fact, it's superb with pork entrees, enchiladas or virtually any dish. If you can't find canned tomatillos in your supermarket, look for Herdez Salsa Verde, Embasa Green Jalapeño Sauce or any green salsa listing tomatillos as a key ingredient.

3 cups canned green Mexican tomatillos, drained
1 1/2 onions
5 - 10 fresh yellow or jalapeño chiles (very hot)
5 - 8 fresh Anaheim chiles (very mild)
1 small bunch cilantro
1 tbsp chicken bouillon
1/2 tsp lemon juice

Wash all chiles and tomatillos and remove stems. In a large Dutch oven, place chiles and tomatillos in about one inch water. Bring to boil and simmer for two to three minutes. Remove from stove and cool for a few minutes. When you can handle the chile mixture, drain off about half the water and mince in the food processor. Put all minced chiles and tomatillos in a large bowl. Dice onions in food processor and stir into chile mixture. Wash cilantro and cut off the longest portion of the stems. Dice remaining part of the plant in the food processor. Stir into salsa. Add lemon juice and bouillon. Stir well. Place in quart size jars and refrigerate. Depending on quantities of chiles you use, this should make about two jars of salsa. It's best if refrigerated at least eight to twelve hours and will keep for several days in the refrigerator.

MARC'S MANGO SALSA TROPICAL

Nina's and my friend, Marc Spahr came to Todos Santos, then a tiny undiscovered town an hour northwest of Cabo San Lucas back in 1986. He came because he wanted to farm and the water there was sweet and plentiful. First thing he did was to buy himself a farm and plant every kind of tropical fruit tree he could get his hands on. Now he grows 20 varieties of fruits and berries, plus 12 types of bananas. Almost all the fruits he grows are used at Caffé Todos Santos, a one-of-a-kind gem of a restaurant he opened in '93.

This unusual, spicy-sweet salsa has to be made with all fresh ingredients. No canned! With its totally tropical taste, it's incredible served with Marc's equally incredible Chicken Flautas (find them in the Appetizer section). Or you can try it spooned over grilled chicken breasts, red snapper, or with carnitas. I swear, you'll think you're in the little latitudes, serving dinner under a palapa at the edge of the Pacific or the Sea of Cortez every time!

1/2 cup mango, chopped
1/2 cup pineapple, chopped
1/4 cup papaya, chopped
2 tsp vinegar
2 tbsp water
1/4 tsp salt
2 cups tomatoes, chopped
1/2 cup white onion, chopped
1/2 cup cilantro, chopped
1/2 cup serrano chile, chopped

Mix all ingredients This should make about two jars of salsa. It's best if

refrigerated at least eight to twelve hours and will keep for several days in the refrigerator.

SANTA FE GREEN CHILE SALSA

This amazing sauce originated in New Mexico, as did Juan Carlos, the grinning, Margarita-guzzling gato (cat) that graces the cover of this book. Like all Mexican food, its roots are both Indian and Spanish. However, its flavors are distinctly different. Try this and you'll taste the difference for yourself. Will it turn you into a grinning gato? I don't know. But this salsa is mouth-watering spooned over grilled chicken breasts and can be substituted wherever enchilada sauce is called for. Makes two cups.

12 - 14 fresh Anaheim or canned whole green chiles
3/4 cup chicken bouillon
1 tsp oregano
3 cloves garlic, minced
1/2 cup sour cream, fat-free sour cream or nonfat yogurt

Using fresh chiles: In a heavy skillet, lightly toast the chiles. Turn them constantly so they don't burn. When cool enough to handle, hold the chiles under cold water. Rinse out seeds and discard stems. Using canned chiles: Rinse and pat chiles dry, discarding any seeds or stems. (The hottest part of any chile is the seeds!)

For both types: Puree chiles in food processor. In medium saucepan, simmer chiles, oregano and garlic in bouillon for twenty minutes, or until sauce has thickened. Immediately prior to serving, add sour cream.

SALSA CHIPOTLE

This salsa is one of my favorites because of its delicious, unique, cooked-over-a-campfire smokey flavor. Chipotle chiles are dried jalapeños which are cooked and canned in adobo. They're quite hot, but with deep, almost mesquite-like flavors that remind me of colonial Mexico, back in the days when Jesuit and Franciscan monks like Father Serra traveled up the peninsula building missions and converting Indians to Catholicism.

These chiles can be found in California supermarkets, or in markets specializing in Mexican or Latin American foods. The sun-dried tomatoes add a definite Alta (that's upper) California flair. Try salsa chipotle over grilled turkey or chicken breasts or spoon it over red snapper while it's baking. It's also great for dipping with chips.

1 1 pound 12 ounce can Italian tomatoes in puree
2 tomatoes
8 sun dried tomatoes, boiled in 1/2 cup water until soft
1 onion, quartered
2 - 8 chipotle chiles
2 cloves garlic, minced
1 tsp oregano
1 tsp cinnamon
1 tbsp distilled vinegar

Core fresh tomatoes and cut into large pieces. Place with Italian tomatoes, onion, chipotles and garlic into food processor. Process until coarsely pureed.

Place the salsa mixture in a medium size saucepan along with oregano, cinnamon and vinegar. Simmer for fifteen minutes. Store in quart jars for up to a week. Flavor actually improves after a day or two. This makes about three cups.

THIN SOUR CREAM SAUCE

This authentic Mexican sauce tops chilequiles, tortilla soup and many enchilada dishes. It's lighter and tastes far better than our traditional American sour cream, but if you don't have the time or the ingredients, or if you're looking for a fat-free sauce, try a mixture of half non-fat yogurt and half fat-free sour cream instead.

1/2 pint half and half
2 tbsp buttermilk

Put cream and buttermilk into a quart jar and mix well together. Cover with plastic wrap and set the mixture aside in a warm place (70 to 80 degrees) for about six hours. Move the sauce to the refrigerator and keep it there overnight. It will thicken and become more solid. Shake or stir well before using. Makes one cup.

THICK SOUR CREAM SAUCE

Thick sour cream sauce is richer and thicker than the thin version. It can be used in place of American sour cream in all Baja Magic recipes. Again, you can substitute fat-free sour cream or a third non-fat yogurt and two-thirds fat-free sour cream for these ingredients.

1/2 pint heavy cream
2 tbsp buttermilk

Put cream and buttermilk into a jar and mix well together. Cover with plastic wrap and set the mixture aside in a warm place (70 to 80 degrees) for about six hours. Move the sauce to the refrigerator and keep it there overnight. It will thicken and become more solid. Shake or stir well before using. Makes one cup.

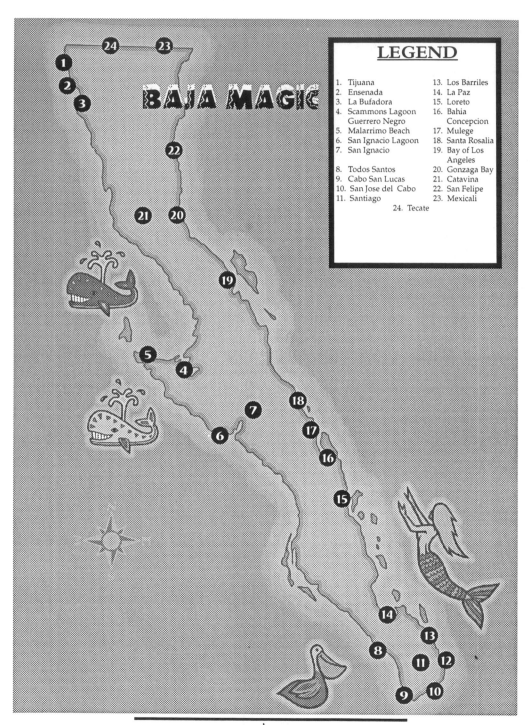

LEGEND

1.	Tijuana	13.	Los Barriles
2.	Ensenada	14.	La Paz
3.	La Bufadora	15.	Loreto
4.	Scammons Lagoon	16.	Bahia
	Guerrero Negro		Concepcion
5.	Malarrimo Beach	17.	Mulege
6.	San Ignacio Lagoon	18.	Santa Rosalia
7.	San Ignacio	19.	Bay of Los
			Angeles
8.	Todos Santos	20.	Gonzaga Bay
9.	Cabo San Lucas	21.	Catavina
10.	San Jose del Cabo	22.	San Felipe
11.	Santiago	23.	Mexicali
		24.	Tecate

BAJA MAGIC

APPETIZERS

Cactus Cat

Whenever I'm headed south on a road trip somewhere in Baja, I love to stop in Ensenada and stock up at one of the local supermarkets where I can save close to 50% on groceries and related items. Avocados cost 10 to 15 cents apiece. They sell the biggest mangos and papayas I've ever set eyes on and their watermelons, tomatoes and Mexican limes (these are smaller and sweeter than their Norteamericano counterparts) are luscious. In the big stores like Gigante and Calimax, you'll find entire deli cases filled with 30 varieties of queso (cheese). I get fresh, hot-off-the-grill tortillas, just-baked bolillos (Mexican hard rolls — oh yum!) and the meat is range-fed and hand cut by a staff of smiling butchers. Like everything else, it's an incredible bargain and ready to be marinated and grilled. I can find everything I need to create a fiesta in Baja — and do it authentically and cheaply.

If you've never traveled in Baja before, let me pass on a few tips. First of all, do some research before you go. Visit the many Baja web sites. Go to the library and the Auto Club. Call one of the Baja travel clubs — Discover Baja or Vagabundos del Mar. By all means, get Mexican car insurance — it's not expensive but it's necessary. If you'll be traveling long distances, have your vehicle checked out stateside before you go. Ask fellow travelers about road conditions. Keep an eye on your map and gas up at a Pemex station (they're all Pemex stations) before you hit a long stretch of empty road. If you do run out of gas or have car problems in Baja and find yourself scratching your head wondering what to do next at the side of a deserted road, don't be surprised when a modern green troque pulls up behind you offering free assistance and gas for sale. Honest! The Green Angels, as they're known, exist solely to help tourists! They patrol all major highways in Mexico — supposedly passing by twice a day. Although most Baja aficionados I know subscribe to the theory that the "worst" roads (read that rutted, gnarly, washboard dirt roads) lead to the "best" places — the Green Angels aren't into off-roading. So be extra-well prepared if you have a hankering to find those "best" places!

One of the amazing things I remember from my growing up years about our camping trips to Baja (and my dad was into bad roads and best places) was the friendliness of the people — Mexicans and gringos alike. Labels and titles and status don't matter south of the border. Whoever you are stateside fades into insignificance as you reconnect with the basic "you." The salt-of-the-earth, easy-going, outgoing, willing to help a stranger "you." Really. I wouldn't even want to count the times Dad got stuck, or ran over a sharp rock and got a flat on our camper and some kind-hearted Mexican rancher showed up out of the blue and helped us out. It was beyond cool.

While you will most likely be trying these recipes in the U.S.A. and shopping at gringo grocery stores, your creations can still taste like you too shopped in Baja. Starting with this section on appetizers, pick out something that makes your mouth water. There's a lot to choose from here; you can offer up any of a variety of munchies to your lucky guests while they're sipping cerveza (that's beer in Spanish), Margaritas or just plain iced tea.

I'm one of those people who could make a whole meal of appetizers. I love them and I'm always adding new ones to my collection. So the choices here range from traditional guacamole (avocado dip) and chips to fiery hot peanuts and include seafood appetizers, quesadillas and an array of other treats. Remember to enjoy yourself. It's a prerequisite to have fun while cooking — and to have even more fun while consuming!

At this point in the book, I think it's time to make a confession. Although I would never be so obtuse as to write a Baja cookbook without including seafood recipes — I don't eat seafood. Never have. Scores of folks in my life have tried to turn that one around, but so far no one has succeeded. I have to give all credit for the tried, true and certifiably delectable seafood recipes in this book to Nina Hazard Baldwin, the book's Seafood Editor, my Twisted Sister, business partner and cohort in crime from the time she was a toddler. She is a Baja chef extraordinaire in her own right. She loves to dive on both the Pacific and Sea of Cortez sides of the peninsula. She looks at the fish and photographs them while her husband, John catches them, hauls them to shore and filets them for her. Then she loves to cook 'em and eat 'em. So, remember that. Not me on the seafood. No way José--Nina!

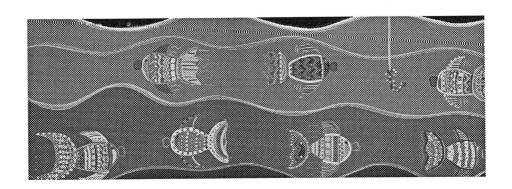

GUACAMOLE & CHIPS

Guacamole (we call it "guac") is a staple in California, the Southwest and throughout Mexico. If fresh ingredients aren't available, you can find prepared guacamole in the deli section of your supermarket.

In Baja we make it by the bucket-full. It's next to impossible to be conservative and make just a little bit of guac with all those cheap avocados around! So when in La Bufadora, we make a lot and then we have it on hand to serve our neighbors as they make the rounds from house to trailer sipping beers on hot summer afternoons. Whether we're there or on the road or camping on a remote beach in southern Baja, we eat it with fresh chips. Or we serve it with our carne asada or carnitas — or whatever we're cooking. You get my drift. Guacamole is a fundamental part of a Baja diet. Get used to it!

Guac:
3 - 4 ripe avocados
2 tsp lemon juice
1 large tomato, diced
1/2 bunch green onions, chopped
1 tsp garlic powder or 2 garlic cloves, minced
1 tsp salt
1/2 tsp pepper
1 - 4 tbsp salsa verde (to desired spiciness)
1/4 cup grated Mexican queso cacique or feta cheese
1 large black olive

Chips:
1 dozen corn tortillas
1/2 cup corn or canola oil
salt to taste

To make the guac: Slice avocados in half and remove seed. Scoop avocado pulp out of the skin using a spoon. Mash avocados in a medium-sized bowl. Add lemon juice, diced tomatoes, green onions, garlic, salt and pepper. Add salsa verde to taste. Stir well, but stop while it's still slightly lumpy. Refrigerate, covered until ready to use. Can be made up to three hours in advance.

To make chips: Slice tortillas into eight pie-shaped wedges. Heat oil in frying pan until a drop of water sizzles when dropped into the oil. Cook tortilla wedges about one to two minutes, browning on both sides.

Desert Java

© Bob Bonn 1997

Tres Amigos

© Bob Bonn 1997

To serve, place guacamole in a bowl in the center of a round serving dish. Garnish with shredded cheese and olive. Surround with chips. Feel free to substitute packaged tortilla chips, made from either yellow or blue corn. This recipe serves four serious munchers or eight casual snackers.

CHILE CON QUESO FAMOSO

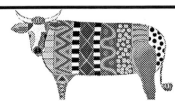

Zesty Mexican seasonings give a great flavor to this hot cheese dip. It's a great party starter, especially during the colder months.

1 pound Velveeta Cheese, cubed
1 cup salsa verde
1 7 ounce can diced green chiles or 2 fresh Anaheim chiles
2 large tomatoes, diced
1/2 red onion, diced
2 tbsp garlic powder
1/2 tsp oregano
1/4 tsp paprika
1 - 2 tsp American chili powder
tortilla chips

In top of a double boiler, cook cheese, stirring constantly until half melted. Add salsa verde, green chiles, onion, tomatoes, garlic powder, oregano, paprika and chili powder. Cook slowly, stirring constantly until cheese is completely melted and all ingredients are blended.

Serve immediately with chips, keeping mixture hot in a chafing dish or crock pot. Check on it and give it a stir from time to time. Serves eight to ten.

SHRIMP IN AVOCADO BOATS

My family was first served this appetizer over 25 years ago at the old Hotel Oceano on the malecón (oceanfront board walk) in Puerto Vallarta. We munched on these (mine were sans shrimp) as we sipped frosty Cokes and people-watched at sunset. Once he figured out how to make them, my dad would whip 'em up on our camping trips to San Felipe over Easter break, using fresh shrimp just hauled in by shrimp boats right off the coast. For those (like me) who don't eat shrimp, the avocado and sauce are perfectly awesome by themselves. Makes me salivate to even think about 'em! This serves eight — and trust me — it's to die for!

4 avocados, cut in half and seeded (do not remove skin)
1 cup red seafood cocktail sauce
1 tbsp lime juice
1 tbsp American chili powder
1 cup small shrimp, cooked and deveined

Place avocado halves on small plates. In small bowl mix cocktail sauce, lime juice and chili powder. Fill the hollow left by the seed with cocktail sauce. Heap shrimp over the top and serve.

CEVICHE GONZAGA BAY STYLE

Gonzaga Bay is a good day's drive south of Mexicali — along several miles of what has historically been washboard road below San Felipe. It's on the east coast of Baja — the desert side of the peninsula, where rains are sparse and the cacti march right on down to the shores of the Sea of Cortez. The climate is warmer than on the Pacific side; the water is warmer and the sunrises over the sea are worth climbing out of bed for. Ceviche originated in places like Gonzaga — places where seafood was plentiful but refrigeration rare. This appetizer is light, low in calories and has become popular all over California, Baja and mainland Mexico because of its subtle but spicy taste. Serves six to eight, depending on their appetites.

2 pounds cubed white fish or bay scallops, raw
5 - 10 fresh serrano or jalapeño chiles (very hot), diced
1 red bell pepper, diced
1 green bell pepper, diced
1 onion, diced
3 ripe tomatoes, diced
1 - 2 cloves garlic, minced
1 bunch cilantro, with stems removed and diced
1 tsp brown sugar
salt and pepper to taste
2 cups lime juice
1/2 cup lemon juice
tortilla chips or gamesas (saltine crackers)

Optional:
2 avocados, peeled and cut into 16 slices and brushed with lemon juice

In a large bowl combine all ingredients except avocados and 1/2 the cilantro. Toss gently but thoroughly, making sure all fish is coated with lemon-lime mixture. Cover and refrigerate one to two hours, stirring occasionally. Fish should become quite white and scallops will lose translucent appearance. (Once this happens, you will know that the lemon juice has "cooked" them and they are quite okay to eat.) Serve in a bowl surrounded with chips or saltine crackers.

Using the avocados: Serve ceviche in individual, lettuce lined bowls. Garnish with avocado slices and additional cilantro.

CONFETTI DIP MARDI GRAS

My mom first came up with the idea for this dip when she, my dad, Aunt Hope and Uncle George were on a month-long camping trip together in Baja and mainland Mexico, right after the highway was finished in 1974. The four of them drove all the way to La Paz and got there just in time for Mardi Gras (a celebration to rival New Orleans' own). They hung around a week or so, camping at various pristine beaches, then caught the ferry over to

Mazatlán (a 16 hour trip) on the mainland and drove home on the opposite side of the Sea of Cortez. Mom and Hope came home with all kinds of new recipes they'd concocted together that trip, and this was one of the first my mom tried on me and Nina. It was obviously named in honor of Mardi Gras and its wonderful array of flavors and colors truly does remind me of confetti. We loved it then and we love it now!

You can make it spicy or mild, depending on whether you include or omit the jalapeños. At parties, I make a bowl of each and put a little red flag on the "hot" bowl to scare off those people who can't take the jalapeños' fire. It's festive and it's an original too.

2 large tomatoes, chopped
1 3 1/2 ounce can sliced black olives
1 3 1/2 ounce can diced green chiles, rinsed
1/4 to 1/2 cup sliced jalapeños (optional)
6 green onions, chopped with tops
1/2 cup grated cheddar cheese
2 tbsp red wine vinegar
3 tbsp olive oil
1 tsp garlic salt
1/4 tsp pepper
tortilla chips

Mix all ingredients in medium sized bowl. Cover and refrigerate at least an hour. This can be made ahead and chilled for up to eight hours. Place in serving bowl on large round platter surrounded by tortilla chips. Then sit back and wait. The compliments will astound you. Serves eight.

RED HOT FLAMING PEANUTS

I was first intro-duced to these fiery little peanuts on an Easter Vacation camping trip to the Meling Ranch, which is a real cattle ranch (that caters to tourists on the side) in the mountains southeast of Ensenada. We caravanned down with four other families and one of the moms turned me onto these nuts. At 15, I was already hooked on hot and I loved to show off my cast-iron palate, so you can imagine how many of these I ate. Believe me, they can be addictive. And dangerous too, as I learned when my mouth (and later my stomach) began to burn like a three alarm fire!

1 tsp corn or canola oil
1 cup raw, unsalted, skinless
peanuts

10 small cloves garlic, minced
1 1/2 tsp each New Mexico chile
  powder and cayenne pepper (hot!)

In small frying pan, heat oil until a drop of water sizzles when dropped into it. Add peanuts and garlic. Fry for about two minutes, turning con-stantly. Reduce heat, add chile pow-der and salt and cook for a minute longer, stirring constantly to ensure that chile powder doesn't burn. Cool before serving. Serves four to eight.

SEVEN LAYER DIP

Twenty minutes north of the Tijuana — San Diego Border is where those of us who are die-hard Charger fans have always flocked every fall to watch them play football. A real local's favorite, this Seven Layer Dip (which, of course, was imported from Baja) can be found at nearly every San Diego Chargers' tailgate party. Just waltz around the parking lot some Sunday afternoon and check out the picnic scene. You'll see! Because this varia-tion uses a layer of shredded lettuce instead of the usual meat, dipping into it is like scooping up a bite of spicy salad. It's lightening-bolt good! Serves eight.

2 16 ounce cans refried beans
(jazzed up with hot pepper sauce if
desired)
1 cup sour cream
1/4 to 1/2 cup sliced jalapeños
(optional)
1 cup salsa fresca
2 cups shredded lettuce
2 cups guacamole
2 cups grated cheddar cheese
sliced black olives and green onions
for garnish
tortilla chips

On a large serving plate, layer first
the refried beans, then sour cream
and jalapeños. Next spread a layer
salsa fresca and a layer of lettuce.
Add guacamole. Top with cheddar
cheese and garnishes. Place it next
to a basket of tortilla chips and
watch it disappear!

JICAMA FRESCA

Jicama (pronounced HEE-kuh-muh) is
a crisp, white root vegetable that is
sold as a snack by vendors all over
Baja and mainland Mexico. Its flavor is
light, zesty and unusual and it makes
a great low calorie appetizer sprinkled
with lime and chili powder. Ask for it in
the produce section of your supermarket and be prepared to be pleas-
antly surprised! While I use it in lots of
recipes, this is your basic Baja version.
Clean, simple and sold on street cor-
ners in clear plastic cups so you can
munch and crunch as you window
shop. Serves eight.

1 - 2 tbsp salt
1/2 - 1 tsp American chili powder
1 - 2 pounds jicama, peeled
1 - 2 Mexican limes, cut in wedges

Blend salt with chili powder in a small
serving bowl. Slice jicama into 1/4
inch by two inch sticks. Arrange on
serving tray with lime wedges and
bowl of chili salt. To eat: squeeze
lime over jicama and dip into salt.

JALAPEÑO JELLY WITH CREAM CHEESE

This tasty and colorful dip makes an excellent Christmas party appetizer because of its intense green glaze. Or sell yourself as an Irish Mexican (I've been known to do that every so often) and serve it up on Saint Patty's Day. The rest of the year, your guests will applaud your creativity as a gourmet chef if you spoon jalapeño jelly over broiled fish. It's as good as it is green — honest!

3/4 cup green bell peppers, diced
1/2 cup whole pickled jalapeño chiles, seeded and chopped
1 1/2 cups cider vinegar
6 cups sugar
6 ounces Certo or pectin
3 - 4 drops green food coloring
1 7 ounce can diced green chiles
6 pint jars with lids
1 8 ounce package cream cheese (reduced fat is fine)
Wheat Thins

Puree green peppers and jalapeños in food processor with 1/2 cup vinegar. Pour mixture into Dutch oven. Rinse food processor with remaining vinegar and pour into pan. Stir in sugar and bring to a rolling boil. Boil one minute. Remove from heat and cool. Skim off any foam. Stir in pectin, food coloring and green chiles. Pour into six pint jars. Keeps up to a month in refrigerator. To serve, scoop three to four tablespoons over softened cream cheese. Serve as a spread with wheat thins.

LOS CABOS CHILI CHIPS

Serve these spicy chips with ice cold Mexican beer (Try Pacifico, Bohemia, Tecate or Corona) and you will swear that you're sitting in a swanky outdoor cafe across from the world-class marina in Cabo San Lucas, that amazing resort at the very southern tip of Baja. As you watch the parade of incoming fishing boats, check out the game fish flags that are flying from their masts. You'll see marlin flags, (plus the red tag and release marlin flags) dorado (mahi mahi) flags, rooster fish flags and others too. Take in the incredible array of upscale

yachts anchored in front of you. Then look out towards Land's End, at the dramatic rock formations that mark the merging of the Pacific Ocean into the Sea of Cortez. Keep your eyes open, so you don't miss that cruise ship as it slides out of the harbor and heads south.

If you strike up a conversation with a couple of locals, they might tell you how the town of Cabo San Lucas, which boasts about 44,000 people is only 30 years old. Its sister city, (the entire area comprised of both towns  and the prime ocean-front real estate in between is now called "Los Cabos") San Jose del Cabo, 27 miles to the north has been around for 260 years and is a major commercial, agricultural and cattle ranching community. It's a lovely, quaint town and home to one of the earliest California missions.

Now that you've had your daily fantasy, combined with a lesson in Baja history, how about trying those Los Cabos Chili Chips? They're great — as an appetizer or on the side with a spicy chicken or fish entree. Makes two cups.

1/2 cup corn or canola oil
2 cups tortilla wedges
1 tbsp American chili powder
1 tsp New Mexico chile powder or cayenne pepper (optional)
1 tsp salt

Heat oil to smoking point in skillet. Fry tortilla wedges, turning constantly until crisp. Drain off excess oil, reduce heat and add chili powder and salt. Cook, stirring constantly for a minute more. Drain and cool on paper towels.

CHILI CHEESE DIP

This is another one of my mom's and Aunt Hope's camping-on-the-beach-in Baja-concoctions. I adopted it as my own and for more years than I care to count, I was asked to bring this dip to every single party I was invited to. Eventually, in self-defense I brought copies of the recipe with me so my friends could make the dip themselves. No matter how much you make, it never lasts more than half an hour. Ever. Honest.

2 16 ounce packages of cream cheese, softened
2 12 ounce cans chili con carne without beans
1/2 cup sliced jalapeños (hot) or diced green chiles (mild)
2 cups grated cheddar cheese
sliced olives and green onions for garnish
tortilla chips

On the bottom of a 9 x 14 pan, spread the cream cheese. Layer the chili on top of it. Next, place sliced jalapeños on top of the chili. If you don't want the zap of jalapeños, use diced green chiles or a mixture of both. Top with grated cheese.

You can make this ahead and refrigerate overnight. Before serving, place in a 350 degree oven and bake for thirty minutes. During the last five minutes of baking, add garnishes and return to oven. Serve immediately with a basket of chips and try to hide your smile as you watch it disappear.

ROLLED TAQUITOS WITH GUACAMOLE

Taquitos, or rolled tacos have been a staple in my diet since I was a toddler. My kids love them too — even cold in their sack lunches. They can be served as an appetizer or as a light lunch. Garnished with guacamole and shredded cheese and offered with salsa on the side, this recipe serves three for lunch or six for snacks. (Short cut: if you're short on time, you can probably find rolled tacos — or taquitos — in the freezer section of your supermarket.)

1 dozen corn tortillas
1/2 cup corn or canola oil
1 cup beef, chicken or turkey filling (in Tacos, Burritos & Tostadas section)
1 cup salsa fresca
1 cup guacamole
1 cup shredded lettuce
1 cup shredded Mexican queso cacique or feta cheese
12 wooden tooth picks

In a small frying pan heat oil until a drop of water sizzles when placed in it. Put a tortilla in, frying lightly on both sides. Make sure the tortilla is still pliable (not crisp) when you remove it from the oil. Place on a paper towel and blot off excess oil.

Put a small amount of filling on one end of the tortilla. Roll up the tortilla and hold together using a tooth pick. Place in metal baking dish and put in oven on low. Repeat process until all twelve rolled tacos are in the oven.

Serve on a bed of shredded lettuce. Top with guacamole and cheese. Serve salsa on the side.

CAFFÉ TODOS SANTOS CHICKEN FLAUTAS

An hour's drive northwest of Cabo San Lucas, on the Pacific side of the peninsula will land you in Todos Santos. Founded in 1724, the town sort of crept along as a remote outpost until the late 1800's when a vast supply of underground water was discovered. Virtually overnight it became a booming agricultural community. Today, in addition to a flourishing cattle ranching business, all kinds of tropical fruits and vegetables are grown in and around Todos Santos.

The most surprising thing of all about the area is the gringo population. It has become a renowned artist colony, thanks to the former Taos, New Mexico resident, Charles Stewart, who became its first expatriate artist back in 1986. These days there are more than 350 American and Canadian creative types who make Todos Santos their home. Why have they come here? Is it because of the Pacific breezes, the climate, its Baja-ness? Partly. But the most-often discussed reason I've heard is that the artists love the light. They say it rivals Santa Fe. Carmel. Or the Bermuda Triangle. I wandered around town not too long ago contemplating the light. It wasn't till I flew home to Southern California that the contrast hit me. The light in all of Southern Baja is luminous. The colors are deeper, brighter. The air is clearer. The ambience is somehow pure. Lively. Real. Just bursting with Baja Magic!

There are two world-class Italian restaurants in town — and — get this — there's the Hotel California. Yes. "The" Hotel California, the one the Eagles sang about in the early 70's. A coincidence? Hardly! Back then Don Henley was a part owner. He may have pulled out of Todos Santos, but I bet he'll be back some day, as the word travels about this place.

Nina's and my friend, Marc Spahr owns the Caffé Todos Santos and has since 1993. A gringo and a self-taught chef, his culinary creations are nothing short of awesome. Everything Nina and I tasted from his restaurant was original and delicious! These flautas differ from their cousins, the taquitos in that these use flour (not corn) tortillas. He marinates them in coconut milk with a hint of curry — and oh man — are they ever good! In fact, these are a must try. ASAP! Serves four.

4 boneless, skinless chicken breasts
12 flour small flour tortillas
2 cups fresh (if possible) coconut milk
1/8 tsp curry powder
1 cup corn or canola oil
1 head Romaine lettuce, shredded
1 cup Cheddar cheese, shredded
1 cup tomatoes, chopped
1 cup guacamole (in Appetizer section)
1 cup thick sour cream sauce, (see in Salsa section) or regular sour cream
1/4 cup Parmesan cheese, grated
salt and pepper to taste
Marc's Mango Salsa Tropical (see in Salsa section)

Simmer chicken in coconut milk until cooked through. Set aside to cool and marinate for about an hour. Then shred chicken and place in bowl with curry and just enough coconut milk to wet. Mix well, adding salt and pepper to taste. Roll chicken in tortilla tightly and fasten shut with a toothpick. Fry in oil just until tortilla is golden brown. Drain on paper towels.

Place three flautas on each plate and cover each serving with shredded Romaine, tomatoes and cheese. Add guacamole and sour cream sauce. Sprinkle with Parmesan cheese and serve with Marc's Mango Salsa Tropical.

MARINATED HOT CARROTS & JALAPEÑOS

These traditional Mexican snacks are not recommended for people with dainty palates! For those of us who can take the heat, they're low in calories and tantalizing. If you're not sure about your aptitude as a chile-eater, try them anyway — just avoid the jalapeños if they start getting to you! Makes about a quart.

10 carrots, peeled and
sliced in rounds
8 - 10 sliced canned jalapeños
3/4 cup cider vinegar
1/2 cup water
1/3 cup olive oil
1 onion, sliced thinly
1 tbsp oregano
1 bay leaf

Steam carrots in microwave or saucepan until slightly crisp. In medium bowl combine carrots, jalapeños, vinegar, water, olive oil, onion, oregano and bay leaf. Set aside in refrigerator for at least eight hours. Will keep up to a week.

ZESTY RELLENO BITES

A friend I used to hang out with in Baja in years past gave me the original recipe for these relleno bites. It's one of those recipes everyone took turns tinkering with and this is the version that has sort of evolved and become our favorite. Beware, however. It's one of those super yummy appetizers that tend to disappear before the chef even has a chance to have one single bite! Serves four to eight.

4 cups shredded cheddar cheese
(set aside 1/2 cup for topping)
4 cups shredded Chihuahua or Jack cheese (set aside 1/2 cup for topping)
2 lb fresh pasilla or ancho chiles (spicy) or 2 lb fresh Anaheim chiles (milder), blistered
or 6 7 ounce cans diced green chiles (mild)
6 eggs, well beaten
6 tbsp flour
1 8 ounce can condensed milk (unsweetened)
2 cups (or 2 7 1/2 ounce cans) salsa verde
queso fresca or feta cheese as garnish

To blister chiles, wash, pat dry and cook over a gas burner, turning constantly until they're evenly charred and stop making popping sounds. Wrap each chile in a moist paper towel to steam. After a few minutes, peel skin off chile. Remove seeds and dice. If using canned chiles, simply spread on a paper towel and pat dry.

Grease a 9 x 14 inch pan. Layer 1/3 of chiles and 1/3 of remaining cheese. Repeat twice, for a total of three layers. Add flour and milk to eggs. Blend well. Pour over chiles and cheese. At this point, the dish can be refrigerated up to 24 hours. Bake at

350 for 30 minutes. Remove from oven, top with salsa verde and remaining cheeses and bake an additional 15 minutes. Cool until warm, cut into one inch squares, serve and watch them disappear!

BAJA CRUISER NACHOS

Nina's and my cousin Susan is a cruise aficionada if I've ever known one. She and her mom, our Aunt Joan, have traveled all over the world on just about every type of sea-going vessel imaginable. Susan brought me this recipe back from her cruise on the Mexican Riviera — which stretches from Cabo San Lucas on the north to Puerto Vallarta on the south. Ships depart Los Angeles at Long Beach, cruise down the Pacific Coast of Baja to Land's End, spend a day in Cabo and then cross the Sea of Cortez to Mazatlán and Puerto Vallarta. After a short stay in each port, the ships turn around and head back up north, returning in a week's time.

While I've never taken a Mexican cruise, I have spent plenty of time in each of those seaside resorts. And I've made Susan's Baja Cruiser Nachos plenty of times too. Onboard the cruise ships, they use blue corn tortillas, which originate in New Mexico, for their nachos. The Indians use this variety of corn to make blue corn tortillas, which have a gray-ish color and taste slightly more robust than regular yellow or white corn tortillas. This cruise ship appetizer is a crowd pleaser. It's unsurpassable when made with blue corn tortilla chips, but regular corn tortilla chips can be easily substituted if you can't find blue corn chips. Serves eight.

2 dozen blue corn tortillas, cut in wedges & fried, or
1 package blue corn tortilla chips
1 cup grated Mexican queso Chihuahua or Jack cheese
1 cup grated sharp cheddar cheese
1/2 cup green onions, diced
1/2 cup sliced jalapeños (hot) or diced green chiles (mild)
1 tomato, diced
1 3 1/2 ounce can sliced black olives

Arrange tortilla chips on oven-proof platter. Top with both kinds of cheese, green onions, chiles, tomato and black olives.

Bake at 350 degrees in oven for ten minutes or until cheese is bubbling. (This can also be microwaved. Time will vary depending on your microwave, but should take from one to two minutes.) Serve immediately.

AVOCADO-CRAB COCKTAIL

According to Nina and everyone else who's tried it, this recipe is a real winner! It's delicately spiced and elegant. If you close your eyes as you pop the first bite into your mouth, it may even make you believe you're basking pool side at a five star resort in Cabo San Lucas or, really anywhere along the Los Cabos strip. If you choose, you can use reduced or non-fat mayonnaise and then sit back and smile as you watch those fat grams shrink. (This part really helps the image of oneself at pool side!) Serves eight.

4 avocados, cut in half and seeds removed
1 pound crab meat
1 tsp hot pepper sauce
1/2 cup celery, minced
1/3 cup mayonnaise
1 tbsp lemon juice
1 tbsp seasoned salt (Spike is good)
pepper to taste

2 heads lettuce, shredded
8 hard cooked eggs, chopped
8 strips pimento
2 lemons, quartered
2 tomatoes, cut in 8 wedges
8 black olives

Dressing:
2 cups mayonnaise
1 tsp tarragon
2 tbsp chopped chives
6 tbsp tomato puree

Flake crab meat and combine with hot pepper sauce, celery, mayonnaise, lemon juice, seasoned salt and pepper in large bowl. Place avocado halves on shredded lettuce. Fill with crab mixture and sprinkle generously with chopped eggs. Garnish with pimento strips, lemon and tomato wedges.

To make herbed mayonnaise dressing, combine mayonnaise, tarragon and chives in bowl. Add just enough tomato puree to make dressing pourable. Serve on the side.

SPECIAL QUESADILLAS MEXICALI STYLE

These quesadillas are absolutely the best. I've loved them and yearned for them for over 20 years, but the only place I've ever seen them on a restaurant menu is in the Imperial Valley, just to the north of Mexicali — right on the border between California and Baja California. They were supposedly created in the early part of this century by the Mexican nationals who farmed on both sides of the dotted line.

Because the raw tortilla dough is deep fried, the resulting quesadillas puff up with air like huge cheese pastries. They're indescribably delicious when smothered in salsa fresca, or just plain if you're salsa-phobic like my son, Derek.

3 cups self-rising flour
1 tsp salt
2 tbsp solid vegetable shortening
(or lard if you're into authenticity)
1 1/8 cups water
12 slices Chihuahua or Jack cheese
2 cups corn or canola oil
2 cups salsa fresca

Cut shortening into flour. Add salt. Stir in water slowly with a fork until a ball of dough is formed. Cover and let sit 20 minutes.

Grease hands with oil. Form dough into 12 balls the size of eggs. Roll or pat out until relatively thin (about the size of a tortilla). Place a slice of jack cheese on one side of each "tortilla." Fold in half and flute edges to seal tightly.

Heat oil in deep skillet until a drop of water sizzles when put in oil. Deep fry quesadillas until golden. They will puff up like turnovers. Drain on paper towels and serve immediately with buckets of salsa.

BLUE CORN QUESADILLAS

This Southwestern or upscale Baja specialty can be modified to be as sophisticated as you like. Use Muenster, Brie or Chevre instead of the Chihuahua or Jack, add some chopped fresh basil and even your most affluent guests will be impressed. Serves eight. Try with a variety of salsas as an accompaniment.

8 blue corn or regular corn tortillas
1/2 pound Chihuahua or Jack cheese, sliced
1/2 pound Mexican queso cacique or feta cheese, crumbled
 cooking oil spray

In small skillet, spray cooking oil. Heat until skillet is medium-hot. Place a tortilla in pan and cook about 30 seconds. Turn over. Place a slice of each type of cheese on one side of the tortilla, fold and continue cooking, turning frequently until cheese is melted. Serve on heated platter with various salsas on the side.

HOT CHAPOTOS

Beach side eateries in Southern California and northern Baja offer deep-fried jalapeño rellenos (usually called jalapeño poppers) like these on their appetizer menus. Lately, they've become so popular that even the grocery stores stock heat'n serve stuffed jalapeños.

This is my version, which I named Hot Chapotos after two wild and crazy guys I worked with on a construction project back in the 70's. They ate the most and the hottest chiles (and drank equivalent quantities of beer) of any people I've ever run into in my life.

We had a crew of over 75 guys on that job. On Friday afternoons at 3:30, someone would make a beer run. Almost on cue, the dynamic duo, Joe and Joe would entertain us with their chile-eating and beer-drinking talents. (Who won? Why — Joe of course!) Later on, some of the other guys would get into contests to see who could hammer a ten penny nail into a two-by-four the fastest, but I was more impressed with the chile-eating. I still don't know how they did it. These are hot, so I don't recommend them for those of you who are fire-sensitive.

12 whole canned jalapeños (seeds in for hot, seeds out for not-so-hot)
12 1/2 x 1/4 inch chunks of Chihuahua or Jack cheese
3 eggs, lightly beaten
1 tsp baking powder
1/2 cup flour
1/4 cup corn flake crumbs
1 cup corn or canola oil

Make an incision in each jalapeño and stuff it with a chunk of cheese. Beat together the eggs, baking powder, flour and corn flake crumbs. Heat the oil in a skillet until a drop of water sizzles when dropped into it. Dip each jalapeño into the egg batter and fry for two minutes on each side in the hot oil. Drain on paper towels and serve hot with lots of iced tea, frosty Coca Cola or cold cerveza.

LA COLA DE LA SIRENA
(MERMAID'S TAIL)

One of the most picturesque beaches in all of Baja is Tecolote Beach, 20 minutes northeast of the city of La Paz on the Sea of Cortez. When Nina and I were kids, we often picnicked there — but in those days the beach was only accessible by boat. Now the paved road goes as far as Tecolote and then stops, dropping you off at a huge stretch of sand populated only by two palapa-style restaurants, (a palapa, in case you don't know — is an open-air structure with a thatched palm roof — usually right on the edge of the sea) the odd camper or two and an abundance of birds, churning fish and other sea life.

On a recent trip, Nina and I cut short our stay in Los Cabos by a day so we could get back to Tecolote Beach, park ourselves under the palapa and just bask in the beauty of it all. It drew us like a magnet. A blast from our long-ago (try 35 years) past. A place still cut off from the hub-ub of life, still spilling over with Baja Magic.

The waiter, Marcello remembered us from a prior visit. A super-friendly guy who loves to brag about his mixed (1/3 Italian, 1/3 African and 1/3 Mexican) ancestry, he couldn't wait to offer us his favorite recipe. He chose this one, he explained, because, after watching us swim, he knew we had both been mermaids in a previous incarnation! He also told us that the mermaids shadow the grey whales on their trek from the Arctic to their birthing grounds in Baja — those same whales who sneak into the bay of La Paz periodically. The mermaids and whales communicate by singing, and they dance together, flipping their tales in unison in the late night, under the watching eyes of the moon and stars.

Try Marcello's recipe from the Palapa Azul. You too will feel like taking a running dive and splashing down in the 86 degree, lighter-than-aquamarine-green water off Tecolote Beach. You too will swim on and on and on, unable to force yourself to go back to land, because you too have become a creature of the sea. A mermaid or merman.

1 can of Sardines, drained and finely diced (or 1 can tuna, drained and shredded)
4 hard-boiled eggs, finely diced
1/2 cup tomato juice
1 large white onion, finely diced
2 - 4 (depending on desired spiciness) marinated jalapeños, finely diced
freshly ground pepper, to taste
salt, to taste
1/2 cup mayonnaise (non-fat is okay)
gamesas (saltines) or
tortilla chips for dipping

Combine sardines, eggs, tomato juice, onion and jalapeños in small bowl. Add pepper, salt and mayonnaise. Stir gently until all ingredients are thoroughly but lightly coated in mayonnaise. Add a little extra if the dip appears too dry. Chill well. Serve scooped onto saltine crackers or tortilla chips. Serves six.

DRUNK SHRIMP

In Spanish, Drunk Shrimp are translated into Camarones Borrachos. This easy-to-prepare shrimp appetizer is lightly spiced with herbs and beer. Its name alone makes for great party chatter and the flavors are guaranteed to live up to the name. My dad and his friend, (and camping buddy) Ben invented it in a very basic form on one of family treks to Kilometer 181 — a deserted (back then — in the 60's) stretch of rugged, spectacular coast accessible only by twelve miles of gnarly washboard, washed-out-in-places road just south of Ensenada when I was a kid. Like many of my recipes, it's been jazzed up over the years. Serve this family specialty as a mid-afternoon snack or with cocktails in the evening — and be sure to tell everyone what it's called!

4 12 ounce cans beer
1 large onion, quartered
1 cup lemon juice
2 tsp celery salt
2 sprigs cilantro
2 tsp salt
2 bay leaves
1 tsp thyme
1 tsp basil
6 whole cloves
dash ground pepper
dash ground cumin
2 pounds shrimp, unshelled
1 cup seafood cocktail sauce -or-
3/4 cup melted butter
toothpicks for use in dipping

Combine beer, onion, lemon juice and spices in large saucepan. Bring to boil. Reduce heat and simmer, covered for ten minutes. Drop shrimp into stock and bring to boil. Reduce heat again and simmer three to five minutes, or until shrimp are pink. Remove shrimp from stock and allow to cool briefly.

To eat shrimp, hot or chilled, simply shell and dip in cocktail sauce or melted butter as desired. Serves eight.

EMPAÑADAS ESPECIALES

This traditional Latin American specialty makes a terrific finger food. The little turnovers fit easily in the palm of your hand and they're stuffed with a variety of delectable ingredients. They're as yummy as they are appealing to the eye. My La Bufadora buddy, Sue, who donated this pastry recipe, has a message for you. She says, "Ladies, put on a colorful skirt, wide belt and peasant blouse, put a hibiscus blossom in your hair (men — try baggy pants and a peasant shirt — no flowers, please) and serve these empañadas on a lettuce-lined platter with salsa on the side. Oh, and be sure to lose your shoes. Then you'll feel and look like a genuine Mexican. All you'll need now is a battered but roadworthy troque!" Sue should know. She lives in Baja full-time. Recipe yields about three dozen.

Filling:
3 onions, finely chopped
2 tbsp corn or canola oil
1 pound ground beef
1/2 cup beef bouillon
1 cup raisins
1 tsp ground cumin
1 tsp oregano
20 pitted green olives, chopped
salt and cayenne pepper to taste
2 hard-cooked eggs, chopped

Sue's Famous Pastry:
2/3 cup plus 2 tbsp solid vegetable shortening
2 cups flour
1 tsp salt
4 -5 tbsp cold water

Cook onions in oil in skillet until translucent. Add beef and brown lightly. Add bouillon, raisins, cumin, oregano and olives. Simmer 30 minutes. Season to taste with salt and cayenne pepper. Remove from heat and stir in eggs. Cool.

Cut shortening into flour and salt until crumbly. Gradually add water, one tablespoon at a time, stirring with fork until pastry is uniformly moistened and cleans side of bowl. Roll pastry on floured surface to 1/4 inch in thickness. Cut into two inch rounds. Place one tablespoon filling on each, fold over and flute edges to seal. Pierce tops with fork.

Bake at 375 degrees fifteen minutes, or until browned. Serve hot or cold, with a variety of salsas.

SHRIMP DIP SAN FELIPE

The Colorado River dead ends where the Sea of Cortez begins. About an hour south of the delta is San Felipe, where the low tides are so low you can walk out half a mile across sand that was underwater just a few hours earlier. Imagine yourself, swinging lazily from a hammock strung up under a palapa at Pete's Camp, which is where we parked our campers back in the 60's. It's still there, too. Putting your book down, gaze out to sea as the tide slithers in towards you. Bait fish jump and pelicans swoop across the warm ocean, alerting the fleet of panga fishermen patrolling offshore to the whereabouts of their family's dinner. You sigh, close your eyes and drift off to dream land. This is perfection.

One of my favorite recollections from our Easter vacations at Pete's Camp was when Nina and I were in high school. Feeling a little restless, and more than a little bit ready to stir up some action, we decided to take the family dog, Victoria for a stroll. It was that magical, mystical time of day right before sunset, when the light is pure gold. As we wandered around camp, we suddenly heard the roar of an approaching aircraft. Soon enough, a single engine plane swooped down out of the sky and roared to a stop on the dirt road right next to us. Mouths hanging wide open, we stared in disbelief as the door to the plane unhinged and out popped a single dad named Steve, his teenage son and daughter. We brought them over to our campsite and they became instant friends with everyone in our group.

The shrimp caught here on the northeast coast of Baja are among the finest anywhere. From San Felipe to Gonzaga Bay, the shrimp boats patrol regularly, scooping up these delectable morsels in their nets. Drive to

the dock at the breakwater any afternoon in your dune buggy (or "sandrail"
as the Arizona folks call them) and you
can buy them fresh off the boats —
just like my parents, Nina and I did over
30 years ago during our Easter vacations. And be sure to check out Pete's
Camp. I don't know if gringos are land-
ing their planes on the dirt roads anymore — but you never know, do you?
Not in Baja!

1 8 ounce package cream cheese
1 cup small cooked shrimp
1 1/2 cups salsa verde
1 tsp Worcestershire sauce
1/2 tsp garlic salt
1 tbsp hot pepper sauce
paprika as garnish
tortilla chips

Mix all ingredients in small ovenproof
dish. Garnish with a sprinkle of paprika. Bake at 350 degrees for fifteen
minutes or until heated thoroughly.
Serve hot with tortilla chips. Serves
eight.

SOUPS

Something Fishy

Both chilled and steaming-hot soups can be found in this section. Gazpacho Rojo, a chilled vegetable soup that originates in Spain is definitely worth serving for lunch or on a hot summer evening. For a different twist, you can try Gazpacho Blanco, its lighter, white Baja California cousin. Many traditional, wonderful Mexican soups are included, as well as some cool, tropical soups and Juan Carlos' favorite, that New Mexico staple, Green Chile.

You'll enjoy the variety of soups presented here throughout the year. The frosty-cold soups are perfect for summer, while the heartier, hot soups will warm you up on the inside when it's cold outside. Be brave and try making one or two of these soups — I especially recommend trying the recipes that sound kind of iffy to you. I swear to you that your adventurous spirit will be rewarded and you (and those for whom you cook) will not be disappointed! So get busy. Pretty soon you'll be acquainted with the renegade who's hiding out somewhere inside your soul! Does this mean that if you make Lentil Soup Borracho — by next Thursday you will have sold everything you own, bought a grungy old pick-up truck — troque, pardon me — and disappeared into the deepest recesses of Baja with only a bottle of tequila to keep you warm at night?! Or, worse yet — if you try your hand at Cantaloupe Soup Acapulco you'll run off to the rain forest the week after — never to be seen or heard from again?!

Beats me.

Your guess is a whole lot better than mine! Whip up a pot of soup and see what happens!

And be sure to send a postcard if you are transformed into an instant expatriate!

GAZPACHO ROJO

Gazpacho Rojo has been a favorite of mine since my mother first turned me onto it back in Madrid, Spain in 1967. We ate it at least every other day and between the two of us, I'm sure we drove every waiter assigned to us nuts as we batted our eyelashes and begged ever-so-sweetly for a copy of the recipe. Our perseverance paid off. Eventually. Here is what we came up with once we got home and did a little experimenting. Served chilled, it's a delightful and healthy accompaniment to a summer luncheon or outdoor barbecue. And it tastes way, way better than you'd expect! This recipe makes about six cups.

1 large onion, quartered
4 cloves garlic, minced
2 bell peppers, quartered
8 medium tomatoes, quartered
1 large cucumber, peeled and chopped
1/2 cup green onions with stems
1/2 cup lemon juice
2 cups tomato juice
1/3 cup olive oil
2 tsp salt
1/2 tsp pepper
1 cup inexpensive white wine

Toppings:
4 hard boiled eggs, diced
1 cup croutons
1 bell pepper, diced
1/2 cucumber, diced
1/2 cup chives

Puree first eight ingredients in blender. Remove from blender and put in very large bowl. Mix remaining ingredients in the blender. Combine with first ingredients in bowl and stir well.

Empty into quart jars and refrigerate at least two hours. This can be kept in the refrigerator for several days. The flavor actually improves with age!

To serve, place a cup of chilled Gazpacho in each of six bowls. In separate small serving bowls, place the diced egg, croutons, diced bell pepper, cucumber and chives. Watch your guests serve themselves, spooning a bit of each condiment onto the top of their Gazpacho. Then sit back and smile politely as they rave about your culinary expertise!

GAZPACHO BLANCO

Gazpacho Blanco is a less robust Baja California version of the original. I first tasted it in a now defunct restaurant in San Jose del Cabo the year before my daughter, Gayle was born. True to my genealogical legacy, I begged the recipe off the waiter. It's every bit as good as the original red gazpacho — just different. Try it with seafood or chicken dishes, or serve with any light summer meal. This should make about six cups of compliment-worthy Gazpacho. And it is guaranteed to make you feel somewhere between down home barefootin' it in blue jeans and evening dress sophisticated — depending on which direction your mood leads you!

1 large cucumber, peeled and chopped
2 cloves garlic, minced
1 1/2 cups chicken broth
1 cup sour cream
1/2 cup plain yogurt
1 cup dry white wine
salt and pepper to taste

Toppings:
2 medium tomatoes, peeled and diced
1/2 cup diced green onions (white part only)
1/2 cup chopped parsley or cilantro
1/2 cup slivered toasted almonds

Puree cucumber, garlic and one cup of chicken broth in blender. Remove from blender and place in large bowl. Puree remaining broth, sour cream, yogurt, wine, salt and pepper. Mix thoroughly with other ingredients in bowl.
Empty into quart jars and refrigerate at least two hours. This can be kept in the refrigerator for several days. The flavor actually improves with age!

To serve, place a cup of chilled Gazpacho in each of six bowls. In separate small serving bowls, place the diced tomatoes, green onions, parsley and slivered almonds. Just as you did with the original Gazpacho Rojo, watch your guests serve themselves, spooning a bit of each condiment onto the top of their soup. Then sit back (one more time) and grin up a storm as they applaud your culinary expertise!

Tres Palmas

© Bob Bonn 1997

Margaritas

© Bob Bonn 1997

AVOCADO SOUP

This rich and delicious soup combines the traditional with the unexpected. It is an easy-to-make chilled soup that looks (and tastes) wonderful served in glass bowls on a hot summer night. Originally inspired by my cousin Susan's cruise down the Mexican Riviera, I've tinkered with it over the years and recreated it into something a little less exotic and a little more down-to-earth. Read that a little more authentically Baja! This soup can be dinner party fare, beach picnic fare or just good eating in the backyard! Serves eight.

4 avocados, peeled and diced
4 cups chicken bouillon
pepper to taste
4 cups whipping cream
4 tbsp cognac
4 tbsp sherry

Puree avocado in food processor with chicken bouillon. Season with pepper. Gradually stir in whipping cream. Chill. Add cognac and sherry immediately prior to serving.

FIDEO TECATE

A border town, Tecate is world-famous for its beer and its health spas. On holiday weekends, rather than sit through nightmarish lines at the border crossings in Tijuana, (Ordinarily the wait to get back into the U.S. is only 20 minutes. On three-day weekends like Memorial Day it can wind up taking nearly two hours to get across!) my friends and I have often taken the longer, but infinitely more scenic route from Ensenada to Tecate. A lesser known fact about that ride through the Guadalupe Valley is that it is quickly becoming the premier wine-producing area in Mexico, the  most famous of its vineyards being the Domeq and the L.A. Cetto Wineries, both of which conduct tours. In winter and spring, I highly recommend making this drive. Recent rains will have made the hillsides lush and green. The mountains are strewn with spectacular rock formations and top out at 4,200 feet.

One of my friends visited one of the trendy yet affordable health spas located in Tecate, just 34 miles east of Tijuana in the mountains back in the early 80's. She brought me back this recipe she'd pilfered from one of the waiters there. Fideo is vermicelli in tomato broth and can be best described as a Mexican or Latin American "spaghetti soup." Offered in place of rice and beans in parts of Baja, mainland Mexico and the Southwest, it's lightly spiced and quite flavorful. A great alternative for those of us who are counting our (groan!) fat grams. Serves six.

3 tbsp corn or canola oil
4 ounces very fine vermicelli
5 very ripe tomatoes
2 cloves garlic, minced
1/2 onion, chopped
3 cups chicken bouillon
4 cups water
cilantro sprigs for garnish

In skillet, heat the oil until smoking. Fry vermicelli in bundles without breaking them up until a deep golden brown, stirring constantly. Drain off excess oil, leaving about one tablespoon in pan. Puree tomatoes with garlic and onion until smooth. Add to fried vermicelli and continue cooking over high heat, stirring constantly until mixture is almost dry. Add bouillon, water and bring to a boil.

Lower heat and simmer until pasta is soft, about 20 minutes. Garnish with cilantro when serving.

CANTALOUPE SOUP BAHÍA CONCEPCIÓN

Just southeast of the steamy subtropical jungle of Mulege, almost two-thirds of the way down the peninsula, lies the incomparably lovely Bahía Concepción. It is one of the most-photographed spots in all of Baja, and justly so. Its pristine white crescent sand beaches surround an equally pristine, breath-takingly beautiful aquamarine bay. From one of our camping trips to the area comes this simple but distinctive chilled soup. The combination of cantaloupe and potato gives it a wonderfully rich flavor and texture. Serve it outdoors in the spring or summer and you'll be able to imagine yourself dining al fresco — under a palapa — on the shore of Bahía Concepción at Santispac Beach. Even if you can't be there, you're still guaranteed to get a flock of compliments. Serves six.

1/2 cup half and half
1 cup potato, cooked, peeled and diced

3 cups cantaloupe, peeled and diced
1/4 cup sherry
salt to taste
nutmeg and lime slices for garnish

Place the half and half, potato and cantaloupe in blender. Puree. Stir in sherry and season to taste with salt. Serve chilled in glass bowls, garnished with nutmeg and lime slices.

CHEESE AND ZUCCHINI SOUP

Have you ever planted a vegetable garden in your back yard, hoping to have a variety of fresh delicacies for your table — on the order of lettuce, cucumbers, tomatoes, maybe eggplant, watermelon and a few zucchinis? Was your garden like mine? By that I mean — did you end up with bushel after prolific bushel of zucchini and precious little else?! Well, this recipe is from one of those summers in my life. I played around with an old recipe of my mom's from Ensenada for cheddar cheese soup and added a few other Mexican delicacies — and a whole lot of zucchini! It makes a perfect light meal served with hot buttered tortillas. Serves eight.

2 cans Campbell's cheddar cheese soup
2 zucchini, cut into chunks
1 cup fresh corn off the cob
2 tomatoes, cored and cut into chunks
1 3 1/2 ounce can diced green chiles
I cup chicken bouillon
1/2 bunch cilantro, stems removed and chopped
1 bay leaf
1 tsp oregano
1 tsp basil
salt and pepper to taste

Combine all ingredients in Dutch oven. Bring to boil, then reduce heat and simmer for one hour. Serve immediately.

ALBONDIGAS SOUP

Albondigas, or Mexican Meatball Soup is a robust, tasty soup that can be served alone as a meal or as a first course. It's delicious and as typically Mexican as tortillas and beans. This recipe came from my mother's collection. In the late 60's, as my dad was finishing up construction on our family's "dream house," she flew off to Guadalajara, San Miguel de Allende and Mexico City with my dad's youngest sister, my Aunt Joan. The purpose of their trip was to decorate the new house. They had a major blast together, traipsing all over the place hunting up beautiful, finely crafted furniture, ordering custom handmade rugs and ferreting out folk art from all the different regions of Mexico. My mom's main goal was to find a hand-carved front door from the mission era. She found one, all right. In San Miguel de Allende. And she had it shipped home, along with the rest of her purchases. My parents don't own that dream house anymore, but I do know that the Mexican door still graces the house where I spent my teenage years.

My mom claims that she combined a hastily scribbled list of ingredients (in Spanish of course) given her and Joan by a waiter in the El Presidente Hotel dining room in Mexico City on that trip with a recipe she conned from a waiter at Caesar's in Tijuana to come up with this soup. If she's telling the truth, then this soup is a hybrid from two internationally famous, historic Mexican restaurants. She modified it some herself, so that it's easier to make. Try it. You're guaranteed to love it! So will everyone else. Serves eight.

2 quarts beef broth
6 corn tortillas, cut in strips and fried
1 1 pound 12 ounce can pureed toma-toes
2 medium onions, chopped
2 cloves garlic, minced
2 tbsp oregano
1 tbsp basil
2 bay leaves
1/2 to 1 cup salsa fresca
1 lb ground beef
1 cup cooked white rice
1 tsp seasoned salt
1/2 tsp pepper

In Dutch oven, place beef broth, pureed tomatoes, half the onion and garlic, spices and salsa. Heat to boiling on high, then cover and reduce heat to low.

In large bowl, mix ground beef with cooked rice, the remaining onion and garlic, salt and pepper. Form into meatballs. Fry in a skillet until done. Drain. Add meatballs to broth and simmer for two to three hours. Immediately prior to serving add the fried tortilla chips. This soup may be kept in the refrigerator several days or part of it may be frozen for later use.

LENTIL SOUP BORRACHO

Uh Oh. Here it is. The concoction that just may transform you into an instant expatriate. Drunken Lentil Soup — now that's a name that really heats up the imagination! Seriously, though — I've never really heard of anyone running off into the wild yonders of Baja after indulging in this soup! In fact, it's superb in cold weather and has been one of my sister's and my favorites forever. (We're still present and accounted for too — most of the time.) The flavor of the beer greatly enhances this usually very sedate, traditional Mexican soup. Serves eight. So come on. Be brave. Try it! I dare you ....

1 pound lentils, rinsed
4 cups beer
2 cups chicken bouillon
2 cups water
1 cup celery, chopped
1 red onion, chopped
2 cloves garlic, minced
1 large tomato, finely diced
1/2 cup lime juice
2 fresh jalapeño or 4 serrano chiles,
1/2 tsp rosemary
1/2 tsp basil
salt and pepper to taste
cilantro sprigs and lime slices for garnish

Combine lentils, beer, bouillon and water in Dutch oven. Bring to boil, reduce heat and simmer. Add celery, onion, garlic, tomato, lime juice, chiles and spices to soup. Cook one hour, or until lentils are tender. If soup appears overly thick, add water until it has reached a desirable consistency. Garnish with cilantro sprigs and lime slices. Then serve and enjoy! Serves eight.

PANCHO'S TORTILLA SOUP

This delectable variation of an old Mexican favorite comes to you straight from Restaurant Pancho's in Cabo San Lucas. When I was asking the owner, Mary Bragg, what she was most famous for, she didn't hesitate one second before telling me, "Why our Tortilla Soup. Of course." Nina promptly ordered some, and since both of us are connoisseurs of tortilla soup, we were curious to see if Mary's would prove to be as memorable as she said.

Guess what?! She was right on. This soup is pure Baja Magic. While most versions I've run across use only one kind of broth, this ones uses two.

One pot of chicken broth and another of Mary's Salsa Ranchera (you can find it in the Salsa section of this book) are combined and poured over crunchy, just fried tortilla strips and garnished with sour cream sauce, fresh avocado chunks and cilantro!

This is a true culinary delight. And if you ever get to Cabo, be sure and visit Pancho's. We ate there two nights in a row on our last trip, and then came back the third just to hang out with Mary and her husband, John. Not only is their food delicious beyond belief, but the restaurant's half palapa and half open air ambience is vintage Baja. And the decor — well, it's as colorful and festive as it comes. And their in-house mariachis play those all-time Mexican favorites like Cielito Lindo, Rancho Grande, La Bamba and Cuando Calienta el Sol like the true pros they are. And, you know what else? You will fall in love with Mary's twinkling eyes and effervescent dis-position. She's the premier wedding consultant in Los Cabos — so if you're in the mood for a Southern Baja wed-ding — Mary's the one to call. As a host, John's no slouch either. He boasts the most extensive tequila collection in all of Mexico, honest! Check him out in the From the Bar section of this book. Serves six.

1/2 chicken
2 quarts water
salt, pepper and other seasonings to taste
12 corn tortillas, cut into strips about 1/2 inch wide
1/2 cup corn or canola oil
2 avocados, cut into chunks
1 1/2 cup Chihuahua or Jack cheese, grated
6 cups of Salsa Ranchera (see recipe in Salsa section)
1 cup thick sour cream sauce or sour cream (see recipe in Salsa section)
fresh cilantro, in sprigs

Cook half chicken well seasoned with water for one hour. Remove chicken and cut into chunks. (You should have about two cups of chicken.)

Deep fry the tortilla chips and drain on paper towels. Divide among six large soup bowls Place chunks of chicken, avocado and grated cheese in each bowl. Pour one cup of salsa ranchera and one cup of chicken broth into each bowl. Float a bit of sour cream sauce on top and garnish with cilantro sprig. Serve immedi-ately and prepare to gloat!

POZOLE

"No. I can't put menudo in my cookbook! I just can't do it. I know, I know. It's traditional. Everyone in Baja eats it. But it grosses me out! I can't bear the thought of eating tripe — or even looking at those slices of white stomach lining floating around lose in my soup bowl! Yuck!"

I couldn't do it. So I improvised and have included instead a "bang-up, kick (you know what) and take names" pozole that I've had tons of fun experimenting with over the years. I like it so hot that only my bravest friends (and Nina of course) can stand it if I make it my way. So I don't let myself go crazy like that very often. I just add lots and lots of salsa on the side. This is truly a Baja favorite, only without the gross stuff that my tender tummy can't tolerate. I promise you that you will love it.

This is a January or February soup. One that will warm your innards on a rainy evening — and leave you feeling full and satisfied, even if you're in Akron, Ohio and not a deserted, windy bluff on the edge of the Pacific Ocean watching the sun sink into the cobalt sea as the last visible pod of grey whales for the day makes their way south in the fading light....

Ah yes. Enjoy this one. I sure do! Serves eight to ten. Try with Special Quesadillas on the side for a meal that's outa of this world. Or for sure outa this country!

2lb. lean pork roast
4 boneless, skinless chicken breasts
3 onions, chopped
4 - 6 cloves garlic, minced
2 - 4 tbsp American chili powder
3 whole cloves
1 - 3 tbsp oregano
6 cups water
4 tbsp chicken bouillon
(or more, to taste)
2 16 ounce cans white hominy
salt and pepper to taste

Garnish:
1 onion, chopped
1/4 cup oregano
1 cup cilantro, chopped
1 cup fresh serrano chiles, finely diced (hot! optional)
a sampler of salsas

In a large Dutch oven or crock pot, place first nine ingredients. Heat to boiling and then cover and simmer for four to six hours. Add hominy and salt and pepper to taste. Cover and cook an additional hour. If soup appears overly thick, add water until it has reached a desirable consistency. Garnish with cilantro sprigs and lime slices.

GREEN CHILE
NEW MEXICO STYLE

This New Mexico staple is famous all over the southwest, the wild west and the Baja region. It's really more a stew than a soup because it's so substantial. It's simple to prepare and the combination of flavors, after simmering together on your stove and filling your house with their aroma, will tantalize you with their magical taste. The cat on the cover of this book, Juan Carlos — well, this is his favorite dish. He, like many of the artists in Todos Santos, came to Baja by way of the great American southwest. Why'd he come? I've heard too many stories to be able to discern which is the "true story." My favorite one, however, is that Juan Carlos, being a very smart gato, got wind of the fabulous fishing down south. And being quite fond of fishing, (and eating fish) he decided that he'd check out Baja and see for himself if it was as awesome as everyone said it was.

Of course then, there's the Margarita theory. Juan Carlos has a real thing about Margaritas. And snakes. And cattle. And cactus. And mariachis. And, of course — the light. He's a natural, a real artist. I really think it was the Baja Magic that got him. Pure and simple. The sum total of all of it. Just like it got me and everyone else I know with a bona fide Baja soul. So try this, in honor of Juan Carlos' previous life in New Mexico or somewhere in the vicinity. He hasn't given it up, so neither should we! Serves eight.

1 1/2 pounds very lean pork, cut in large chunks
4 3 1/2 ounce or 2 7 ounce cans diced green chiles
2 medium onions, chopped
2 cloves garlic, minced
1 tbsp corn or canola oil
2 quarts beef broth
2 tbsp oregano
1 tbsp basil
2 bay leaves
1/2 to 1 cup salsa verde
1 tsp Worcestershire sauce
1 tsp seasoned salt
1/2 tsp pepper

In large Dutch oven saute pork, green chiles, onions and garlic in oil. Stir in beef broth and all other ingredients. Cook over medium high heat until boiling. Cover, reduce heat and simmer for two to three hours. This soup may be kept in the refrigerator several days or part of it may be frozen for later use.

SALADS

Desert Dancin'

Customarily, Mexican food is served with a side of refried beans and Mexican rice. In Baja, you will all-too-often find that canned peas have been added to your rice — a culinary and geographic oddity. Let me set the record straight right here. I'm not big on canned peas. In fact, I'm not big on any kind of peas whatsoever. Neither is Nina and neither is our dad. When we were growing up he told our mom they were a right-handed vegetable. Since she was the only non left-hander in the family, she got to eat all the peas. She liked them — the fresh ones anyway. She doesn't like canned peas and she doesn't get Baja's obsession with them anymore than I do.

Back to the beans and rice. While I love them, I prefer salad. In fact, I'm a serious salad-eater from way back. My love of the fresh, crisp greens is hereditary, I'm certain of it.

There is a story about my grandfather that illustrates this. When he was in his mid-80's he went on a camping trip across Northern Baja with his octogenarian buddy Erle Stanley Gardner, which was chronicled in the book, **Mexico's Magic Square**.[1] Now Mr. Gardner was one of the original Baja Aficionados. He was also a well-known author and Hollywood celebrity. (In case you're too young to remember, he was the creator of the "Perry Mason" TV series.) He and Pappy were, after all, kindred spirits. In this book he explains his astonishment as Pappy, (everyone called him Pappy — even Erle!) as he was called, broke open the first of several cases of lettuce on the first night in camp. He emphatically did not want to be caught out in the wilderness without his evening salad. Sure enough, the old guys enjoyed huge salads with their dinners every night.

A decade or so later, my parents went on a month-long camping trip down the west coast of mainland Mexico with my Aunt Hope and Uncle George. My mom came home shaking her head. She couldn't believe that my dad's kooky sister had stashed two cases of lettuce and one of cabbage in her motor home so that she wouldn't be without her salad in the evening! Didn't she know, my mom wondered, that they grew lettuce and cabbage in Mexico?! Maybe not. Or maybe she was merely helpless to change the imprinting in her genes! She was Pappy's daughter, after all.

My goal in this section is to provide you with a variety of salads to enhance your menus, so that you can try a different one with each main course you prepare. In honor of our lean times, all salads use reduced amounts of oil, and in some cases, no oil whatsoever. One ingredient I specify often that you may be unfamiliar with is jicama (hee-KUH-muh). It's a lightly sweet and crispy root vegetable that you should be able to locate if you ask the produce manager of your local grocery store.

So get creative. Maybe — just maybe if you decide to rent yourself a motor home and travel Baja, you'll have become so addicted to eating salads with your Mexican food that you too will bring along your own cases of fresh lettuce and cabbage! But then, maybe not. After all, you're not related to Pappy or Hope, are you?!

[1] **Mexico's Magic Square** was written by Erle Stanley Gardner and published by William Morrow & Company, Inc., New York, 1968. Other Baja travel books he wrote ibn the 60's are **Off The Beaten Track in Baja**, **The Hidden Heart of Baja**, **Hovering Over Baja**, and **Hunting the Desert Whale**. For a real treat and a tried-and-true taste of Baja back then, look for them in your local public library.

JICAMA PICO DE GALLO

Pico de Gallo (pronounced GUY-yo) is half salsa and half salad. What makes my recipe unique is the jicama (see previous page). Served on a bed of lettuce, this side dish is great with Fajitas or most chicken and fish entrees. It's a Baja traveler's dream because all the ingredients can be purchased fresh at any roadside frutería. Serves eight.

3 cups jicama, peeled and diced
1 green bell pepper, seeded and slivered
1 red bell pepper, seeded and slivered
10 radishes, sliced
1 medium onion, thinly sliced
1 cucumber, peeled and diced

Dressing:
1/4 cup olive oil
1/4 cup red wine vinegar
1 tsp oregano
salt and freshly ground pepper to taste.

Combine jicama, peppers, radishes, onion and cucumber. Mix together oil, vinegar and oregano. Pour over vegetables and mix lightly. Add salt and pepper. Toss gently and serve on chilled plates.

WILTED CABBAGE SALAD

I love Wilted Cabbage Salad. Nina and I created this recipe through trial and error copy-catting from our favorite Mexican restaurants in North San Diego County and a couple in northern Baja, which all serve some variation of cabbage salad with their meals. I guarantee that you too will love it. It's delicious, it's light and it's real change of pace from beans and rice. Serves eight.

2 small heads shredded cabbage
2 cups chopped celery
3 tomatoes, diced
12 radishes, finely diced
2 cloves garlic, finely diced

Dressing:
1/3 cup cider vinegar
1/3 cup corn or canola oil
1/2 tsp finely ground basil
1/4 tsp finely ground oregano
salt and freshly ground pepper to taste

In a large bowl, toss together chopped cabbage, celery tomatoes, radishes and garlic. Refrigerate for up to three hours. Just prior to serving, mix vinegar, oil and spices in a small bowl. Heat for 45 - 60 seconds in a small saucepan or in the microwave, until hot. Pour over cabbage salad, toss and serve immediately.

SPANISH RICE SALAD SANTIAGO

This is an unexpected and original way to serve rice. My mom and dad first turned us onto it after a trip to the Santiago Zoo when my kids were really little. Not only does Santiago have the only zoo in all of Baja, but it's also a lovely farming community situated on a pair of hills separated by a shallow, palm-laden canyon. It's located two miles north of the Tropic of Cancer, just off Highway 1 and a bit northwest of Cabo Pulmo. The roadside eatery where we first had this salad had loaded it up with plenty of canned peas. We, however, took it upon ourselves to lose those peas when we recreated the recipe at home!

Try this vegetable-laden, healthy salad with cold meats or any chicken dish for a light dinner. I'm sure you'll love it as much as my family does. Serves eight.

4 cups chilled, cooked white rice
1 cup chilled, thinly sliced cooked carrots
1 cup chilled, cooked cauliflower-ettes
1 large tomato, chopped
1/2 bunch green onions, sliced white part only

Dressing:
1/2 cup corn oil
1 tsp onion juice
1/4 cup wine vinegar
2 tsp celery seeds
1 tsp dry mustard
1 tsp sugar
salt and freshly ground pepper to taste
1 3 1/2 ounce can sliced black olives, drained as garnish

Combine rice, carrots, cauliflower-ettes, tomato and green onions in large salad bowl. Combine oil, vinegar and onion juice, vinegar, and all spices in small jar. Shake well. Pour over salad and toss lightly. Garnish with black olives.

AVOCADO TOMATO SALAD

I created this recipe on a camping trip to Bay of L.A. with my kids and their dad because I'd forgotten to pack any vegetable or olive oil in our motor home. Since we'd shopped in Ensenada on our way south, I did have plenty of avocados, so I decided to let the natural oils inherent in the avocados act as my salad oil. It worked! They blended with the other ingredients to make create a remarkable and delicate salad. For a dish that started out as a semi-accident, this turned out to be really, really good. It serves eight.

4 large ripe avocados
8 tomatoes, diced
2 onions, diced
1 green bell peper, diced
6 large radishes, diced
4 cloves garlic, minced
1 large bunch cilantro with stems removed & diced
 Dressing:
1/2 cup lime juice (Mexican limes are the best! They're sweeter than the gringo version!)
1 1/2 tsp seasoned salt
freshly ground pepper

To line plates:
1 large head romaine lettuce

Cut avocados in half. Remove seed and peel each half. Cut into one inch chunks. Place in medium sized bowl with tomatoes, onion, red and green bell peppers, radishes, garlic and cilantro. Sprinkle with lime juice, salt and pepper.

Toss gently. Refrigerate, covered up to three hours. Line chilled salad plates with romaine leaves. Spoon avocado-tomato mixture on top of each bed of lettuce.

AUNT HOPE'S FIRST-NIGHT-IN-CAMP COLE SLAW

I used to love going camping with Aunt Hope and Uncle George. Why? Hope made the best salads around (it was genetic, remember?) and George used to sneak out in the bushes with me nd we'd smoke cigarettes and gossip like buddies together. No — I don't smoke anymore and George isn't around to hang out with anymore — but I can still make Aunt Hope's Cole Slaw and be instantly transported three decades back in time to some deserted Baja beach at the end of a dusty day of driving. She'd make it before we left home and serve it with my mom's Chilequiles (you can find these in Enchiladas & Rellenos) or something else made ahead of time. It didn't matter what she served it with. It was a tradition and it was always the best cole slaw I ever ate! Still is.

Try it and you will be amazed — even if you can't abide cole slaw. Hers is unique and guaranteed to disappear in record time. Whenever I serve it to a group, it never lasts long enough for second servings. Try it with just about anything — a beef or chicken dish, Chilequiles — whatever you're in the mood for. Just be sure you have plenty of ice cold beverages on hand to wash the road dust from the back of your tongue! Serves eight, más o menos.

1 extra large or 2 medium heads, cabbage, shredded
(but not too finely)
1 - 2 bunches green onions, sliced all the way to the ends
2 8 ounce packages of slivered almonds, toasted until
lightly browned
1/2 cup mayonnaise
(non-fat is okay)

1/2 cup Durkee's Sauce (this is crucial — so search it out!)
coarsely ground pepper

In small bowl, mix together mayonnaise and Durkee's sauce. Set aside. In very large bowl, place cabbage, onions and dressing. Wash your hands and use them to thoroughly mix everything. Move to serving bowl and top with slivered almonds and pepper. Refrigerate from two to 24 hours. It will keep for up to three days in the refrigerator. Watch out! You'll catch people eating the left-overs for breakfast. I do!

ENSALADA CHILENO BAY

Nina maintains that the best beach in all of Los Cabos is at the Hotel Cabo San Lucas. It's called Chileno Bay and it's famous for its underwater rock formations and awesome diving. Although I don't scuba dive, I do snorkel and I can vouch for Chileno Bay being jam-packed with wildly colored tropical fish.

This salad was inspired by a trip our family took to Cabo when I was seven months pregnant with Derek. We stayed at the Hotel Cabo San Lucas and swam in Chileno Bay every day for nearly a week. The water was heavenly, especially to someone as awkward, overloaded and overheated as I was! Only underwater did I feel graceful, buoyant and cool!

In hot weather like they have in Cabo during the summer months, a crunchy, cooling tropical salad like this one is a real delight. Anytime of year it's an ideal companion to hot, spicy dishes. The medley of tangy fruits and vegetables will not only surprise and delight your palate, but it may even get you started believing you've just come in from spending a day snorkeling Chileno Bay. Or perhaps you've just gotten back from a long day of fishing off the coast of Los Cabos. As you take your first bite of this salad, you'll look across the patio of the outdoor restaurant of the Hotel Cabo San Lucas and marvel at the dimming colors of the sunset. You'll relive the day's events, seeing again in your mind the plethora of deserted Robinson Crusoe islands, the crystal clear aquamarine water just teeming with abundant, colorful undersea life. And you will smile. It doesn't get any better than this! Serves eight.

2 heads iceberg, butter or romaine lettuce (or combination)
1 1/2 cups jicama, sliced in strips
1 red onion, sliced
1 grapefruit
2 oranges
1/2 pound cherry tomatoes, halved

Cumin Dressing:
3 tbsp cider vinegar
2 tbsp lime juice
6 tbsp olive oil
2 cloves garlic, minced
1/2 tsp ground cumin
1/4 tsp crushed red pepper
salt and freshly ground pepper to taste
1 large avocado as garnish

Mix lettuce and jicama in large salad bowl. Arrange onion rings on top. Peel grapefruit and oranges, removing all white membrane from sections. Arrange with tomatoes on top of onions. Cover and chill for one to two hours.

To make Cumin Dressing, combine vinegar, lime juice, oil, garlic and spices in food processor. Whirl until blended. Just prior to serving, peel, pit and slice avocado. Place on top of salad. Pour on dressing and toss gently. Serve immediately.

MOLDED GAZPACHO SALAD

This recipe is a favorite of my mother's. It's an exotic salad with a Spanish heritage. Molded Gazpacho Salad is simple to prepare, but delectable — and elegant enough to grace the table any ladies' luncheon in Beverly Hills or La Jolla. Or perhaps, like me, you'd rather be sitting on the terrace of a remote Baja resort like Punta Pescadero on the East Cape between La Paz and Los Cabos watching the iguanas playing and sunbathing on the rocks leading down to the beach. Either way, you will enjoy this exquisite salad. It's fat-free and serves eight.

1 envelope plain gelatin
1 1/2 cups tomato juice
1/2 cup red wine
1 large tomato, chopped
1 cucumber, peeled and chopped
1 green bell pepper, seeded and chopped

2 tbsp diced green chiles
1/4 cup green onions, sliced
2 cloves garlic, minced
salt and freshly ground
pepper to taste
romaine leaves, rinsed and dried

Soften gelatin in 1/4 cup warmed tomato juice. Heat remaining juice until almost boiling. Add gelatin mixture and stir until dissolved. Add wine, vegetables and seasoning. Pour into a one quart mold. Chill overnight. Unmold on a platter lined with romaine leaves.

MARINATED VEGETABLE SALAD

Marinated Vegetable Salad is a crowd pleaser any time of the year. Healthy and easy to prepare, it gets an unexpected Baja flavor boost from the tangy salsa verde. Serves eight.

1 zucchini, thinly sliced
1 cucumber, thinly sliced
1 green bell pepper, seeded and slivered
1 onion, thinly sliced
2 tomatoes, cut into thin wedges
1 7 ounce can black olives

Dressing:
1/4 cup olive oil
1/4 cup lemon juice
1 tsp garlic powder
1/2 to 1 cup salsa verde
salt and freshly ground pepper to taste

Combine vegetables together in salad bowl. Prepare dressing by combining oil, lemon juice, salsa verde, garlic powder, salt and pepper in jar. Shake well. Drizzle dressing over salad. Toss gently. Cover and chill one hour before serving to blend flavors.

WATERMELON FRUIT SALAD

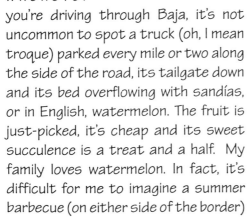

In summer and fall, whenever you're driving through Baja, it's not uncommon to spot a truck (oh, I mean troque) parked every mile or two along the side of the road, its tailgate down and its bed overflowing with sandías, or in English, watermelon. The fruit is just-picked, it's cheap and its sweet succulence is a treat and a half. My family loves watermelon. In fact, it's difficult for me to imagine a summer barbecue (on either side of the border)

without a scooped-out watermelon filled with fruit. The avocado dressing suggested here is a rich, Baja-style change of pace. If you prefer a leaner dressing, try adding an eight ounce container of non-fat fruit yogurt instead. Serves ten.

1 large watermelon, well chilled
1 honeydew melon and/or cantaloupe, scooped into balls
1 cup seedless grapes
1 cup peaches and/or mangos, diced
1 cup strawberries, halved
1 apple, diced
1 cup sliced bananas, sprinkled with lemon juice
1/2 cup chopped walnuts

Dressing:
1 cup whipping cream (fat free or low fat is okay)
2 tbsp powdered sugar
1/2 tsp salt
2 avocados, halved, seeded, peeled and mashed
1/2 cup pineapple juice
1 tsp finely chopped candied ginger

Trace a zigzag pattern horizontally around the top third of the watermelon. Cut through melon with sharp knife, removing top. Scoop out all the watermelon flesh except a shell one inch thick. Scoop removed watermelon into balls.

Combine all fruit and walnuts in the watermelon bowl. Chill until ready to serve.

To make dressing, whip cream with powdered sugar and salt. Blend avocados, pineapple juice and candied ginger until thick and creamy. Fold into whipped cream mixture. Pour over salad and toss gently. Serve.

TEAQUE SLAW

My friend Leslie was raised in New Mexico and then in El Centro, just a few miles from the Mexican border town of Mexicali. A wife of one of the bruseros (or farm hands) who worked for her dad, passed this recipe on to Leslie's mom a number of years ago. The first time she made it, Leslie explained that it's better the second day — and my birthday was the next day — so she made it the day ahead. The problem was, by the next morning it was long gone! There were five of us staying in our La Bufadora house, and even though she made a double batch, between us, we annihilated it! While nothing like Wilted Cabbage Salad or Aunt Hope's First Night in Camp Coleslaw, this slaw (pronounced Tay-AH-kay) is every bit as good. And just as simple to make too. Try it with a Carne Asada Barbecue and you will be amazed! This serves six, but obviously not six of us!

1 large head cabbage, shredded
1 lb Chihuahua or Jack cheese, grated
2 large tomatoes, chopped
1 large white onion, chopped
2 - 3 fresh jalapeños, chopped (canned can be substituted)
1/4 cup cilantro, chopped

Dressing:
1/4 cup olive oil
1/4 cup red wine vinegar
1 tsp oregano
salt and freshly ground pepper to taste.

"THE" ORIGINAL TIJUANA CAESAR SALAD

Did you know that the Caesar Salad originated in Tijuana? Yes. It did. I swear. At Caesar's Restaurant on Avenida Revolución (the main drag in TJ). As a matter of fact, my mother swears this is their original Caesar Salad recipe. Unfortunately, I'll never be able to check it out, because Caesar's closed their doors a few years back. But their famous salad will live on for decades to come, as in elegant restaurants all over Baja and mainland Mexico, white-jacketed waiters continue to slide carts alongside diners' tables and whip these salads together in front of their astonished patrons with great pomp and circumstance. The Caesar Salad is an edible art form in Mexico and one you should go out of your way to try in your travels south of the border.

A few words about Tijuana. Did you know it boasts the busiest border in the entire world?! True! It's also the largest city in Baja, with a population estimated (read that guess-timated) at 1.5 million. It hit its stride as a border city in that interesting span of time from 1920—1933 when Prohibition eliminated legal partying in the U.S. All of a sudden cantinas (bars) and casinos sprang up all over the place as the gringos flocked to Tijuana to play. When Prohibition was repealed, the government made Tijuana into a duty free port and it quickly became a destination for world class shoppers. These days you can buy Cuban cigars — legally there as Aeromexico flies to Havana from Tijuana daily. Do the gringos buy them? You bet they do!

Back to the salad. Nowadays anybody can buy bottled Caesar dressing and whip together a Caesar Salad in just a

few minutes. No big deal. But — if you want to try the "real thing," try this recipe. It's been around a lot longer than I have and it has achieved universal fame. Deservedly so. Trust me, it's more than worth the effort, even if you make it in the kitchen and not tableside! Serves six.

1 large or 2 small heads romaine lettuce

Croutons:
6 slices sour dough bread
1 stick butter, melted
1 tbsp parsley
1 tbsp garlic powder

Dressing:
1 - 2 tsp anchovy paste
1/3 cup lemon juice (fresh if possible)
1/2 cup olive oil
1 tsp Worcestershire sauce
1/3 cup grated Parmesan cheese (fresh if possible)
2 cloves garlic, minced
salt and freshly ground pepper to taste
1 coddled (boiled 1 minute) egg - (optional)

To make croutons, preheat oven to 325 degrees. Cut bread into half inch chunks. Melt butter with parsley and garlic. Toss with bread until evenly coated. Place on baking sheet and bake until crisp and lightly browned, approximately 20 minutes, turning when half-cooked. Cool on paper towels.

To make dressing, combine anchovy paste, lemon juice, olive oil, Worcestershire Sauce, Parmesan cheese, minced garlic, salt and pepper in jar. Shake well until mixed. Refrigerate at least an hour.

To make salad, rinse romaine leaves and tear into bite-sized pieces. Place in chilled salad bowl. When croutons have completely cooled, add them to salad. Immediately before serving, break coddled egg into dressing, pour over greens and toss gently. Serve immediately.

CHOPPED MEXICAN MEDLEY SALAD

This tangy, crunchy salad is "to die for." Its combination of northern and southern Baja flavors makes it perfect with spring and summer meals. It's a one-of-a-kind subtropical treat, no doubt about it! Where did it come from? Me! I made it up one creative afternoon in my Buf house when I was wondering how to use up the over-abundance of fresh produce Nina and I had alternately purchased at Calimax! We had a big fiesta that night and everyone there swore it was a true Baja-lovers delight! Serves eight.

1 1/2 heads romaine lettuce, chopped
1 1/2 pounds jicama, peeled and finely diced
6 seedless oranges, peeled and chopped into squares
2 red onions, finely diced
1 medium bunch cilantro, stems removed & finely diced
4 stalks celery, finely diced
1 large bell pepper, finely diced

Dressing:
1/3 cup olive oil
1/3 cup fresh Mexican lime juice
3 tbsp red wine vinegar
3 tbsp orange marmalade
1/4 cup salsa verde
1 tsp garlic powder
salt and freshly ground pepper to taste

Combine all salad ingredients in a large bowl. Chill in refrigerator up to four hours. Right before serving, add salad dressing ingredients, one at a time to the salad. Toss lightly and serve.

CELIA'S SUMMER NOPALES SALAD

Celia owns one of the restaurants in La Bufadora. Let me tell you — not only does the lady know how to cook, but she is a veritable fount of information on how to get along in Baja. She understands the culture, she knows the rules, and if she likes you, she may even give you a pointer or two on how to play the game.

When I approached her to ask for a recipe to put in this book, I was hoping she'd give me her recipe for flan, a Mexican custard that she makes better than any I've ever had. (Except in Todos Santos — and I got that recipe!) Still, Celia's is so good my son salivates like one of Pavlov's dogs whenever anyone mentions it! But she's hanging on to that one. If you want to try it — along with her ribs, nachos and her Monstrous Margaritas — you'll have to visit us in La Buf and go to her restaurant yourself. (I could think of worse things to do!)

You can pick the nopales (tender, young prickly pear shoots) yourself in spring and early summer if you live in the southwest. Or, if you have a Hispanic market near your home, you can buy fresh nopales already cut and cleaned in the produce section or buy them canned. Either way, you will be able to make this festive, original and surprisingly delicious salad for yourself. I know it sounds pretty weird to you, but it's vintage Baja — so you have to try it! If not at home, then at Celia's.

2 pounds of nopales (tender, young prickly pear shoots), cleaned and cooked
1 tbsp salt
1 tsp pepper
1 tbsp garlic powder
1/2 onion
2 quarts water
2 onions, chopped
4 stalks celery, chopped
1/2 bunch cilantro, chopped
3 large tomatoes, diced
salt and pepper to taste
2 cups shredded mozzarella cheese
1/2 cup Parmesan cheese

Dressing:
1/2 cup olive oil
1/2 cup red wine vinegar
1 tsp oregano
salt and freshly ground pepper to taste.

If using freshly picked nopales, soak in water until thorns are soft, then remove with the point of a knife. Cut into strips one inch long. Place in Dutch oven and add water, salt, pepper, garlic powder and onion. Heat to boiling and simmer 20 minutes. Drain and wash them, discarding all excess liquid. (Note: Only canned nopales are pre-cooked. Fresh store-bought nopales come cleaned but must be cooked.)

Put nopales in salad bowl with chopped onion, celery, cilantro and tomatoes. Toss with salad dressing and mozzarella cheese. Add salt and pepper to taste and chill. Immediately before serving, top with Parmesan cheese.

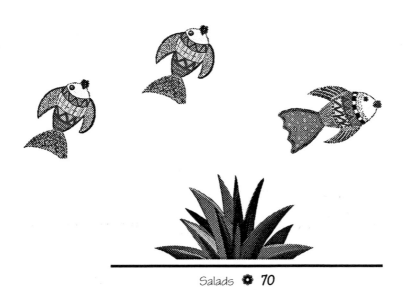

SALADS THAT MAKE A MEAL

© Bob Bonn 1997

Summer Fun

I confess — I like few things better than going out to lunch. It has something to do, I believe, with my *genetically inherited salad addiction!* Give me an innovative lettuce-based creation, a bottomless glass of iced tea and a good friend — and I am one happy lady.

My sister Nina loves to go out to lunch as much as I do. Not only did she inherit Pappy and Hope's salad addiction, but she and I also inherited (from whom we're not entirely sure because no one from the older generation will admit it) a serious salsa addiction. And, in differing levels of intensity, we've both inherited from our mom the passion for visiting a restaurant, ordering different, but equally luscious-sounding salads, sharing bites and analyzing the ingredients while drinking copious amounts of iced tea (or Diet Coke in her case).

While eating, we indulge in what our father calls the "wandering fork" syndrome. This means we feel free to dive into each other's food without making any big fuss about it! We share and then we compare notes. If we're especially impressed by one of the salads we ordered, we check out the ingredients with our server. Then one or both of us will go home and experiment with the recipe — always changing a few things so we can indulge our creativity and at the same time avoid getting ourselves in trouble.

While most of these recipes in this section are derived from genuine Mexican dishes, two or three came from our forays into Southern California Restaurant-Land. (Will I let you know which ones? Maybe — but you can't expect me to divulge all our secrets now, can you?!)

Fix one of these salads for your best friend, your mate, your entire family or for a crowd. They're all suitable for either lunch or dinner, depending on your appetite and preference. And don't forget the pitcher of tooty fruity iced tea. Somehow it imparts an exotic, tropical mood to your culinary experience.

And, for the utmost in dining pleasure — pick a warm day and dine outdoors with a vase of fresh flowers on the table. Take off your shoes so you can wiggle your toes in the grass. Put on some Mariachi or Flamenco guitar music. Or something soothing and mystical from the Andes of Perú. As you dip your fork into your salad, picture yourself on a tiled terrace high above the sea. Listen to those waves as they break on the rocks below you. Inhale the aroma of Mexico. Look up to the skies and imagine a formation of pelicans banking around the corner of the bay below you. Sigh deeply and relish that first bite as the magic of Baja flows through your veins.

Margaritas for Two

© Bob Bonn 1997

Best Friends

TACO SALAD

No, this is not a replica of the taco salad that arrives in a greasy bowl made from a deep-fried flour tortilla and contains more calories than most adult women are supposed to consume in a 24-hour period! This recipe is lighter and more authentically Baja. It makes an outrageous lunch or light dinner for two hungry people. It can be made with either beef, chicken or turkey, the recipes for which can be found in the Tacos, Burritos and Tostadas section of this cookbook. Vary the salsas (use either ready-made or a recipe from this book) to suit the meat and your mood both.

1 head lettuce, torn into bite sized pieces
1 large tomato, diced
1 3 1/2 ounce can sliced olives, drained
1/2 bunch green onions, chopped
1/2 cup pinto beans from can, rinsed and drained
1/2 pound shredded beef, chicken or turkey

Dressing:
1/4 cup salsa of your choice
1/2 cup Italian salad dressing
salt and freshly ground pepper to taste

Garnish:
1 avocado, peeled and sliced
1 cup Mexican cacique, feta or cheddar cheese, grated
1 1/2 cups tortilla chips

On the bottom of a large salad bowl, layer shredded meat, pinto beans and lettuce. Top with olives, green onions, salsa, and tomatoes. Refrigerate up to one hour.

In a small bowl mix salsa and salad dressing. Just prior to serving, Add avocado, grated cheese and tortilla chips as top layer. Toss salad gently and serve immediately.

HOT CARNITAS SALAD

Oh boy, oh boy, oh boy. I do love Hot Carnitas Salad. (Actually I love carnitas period. So does Nina.) The combination of flavors is original and it's a delicious, satisfying meal without being heavy. Even if you aren't a pork lover — be courageous and give this recipe a try. It's not fatty at all. Trust me — you'll be astonished and you'll do yourself proud. The recipe for carnitas is in the Carnitas, Fajitas and Carne Asada Barbecues section of this cookbook. Serves two hungry people for lunch or a light dinner.

1 head romaine, torn into bite size pieces
1 tomato, diced
1 avocado, peeled and sliced
1/2 small can sliced black olives
1/2 bunch green onions, chopped
6 radishes, sliced
1/2 pound carnitas
1/4 cup salsa verde

Dressing:
1/2 cup thick sour cream sauce (use fat-free sour cream if desired)
1/4 cup Mexican lime juice
2 tbsp cup olive oil

1 tsp basil
salt and freshly ground pepper to taste
1/8 inch tortilla strips, fried (from 6 tortillas) as garnish

Use hot, freshly made carnitas or heat left-over carnitas in saucepan or microwave until steaming. On the bottom of a large salad bowl, layer carnitas, olives, green onions, radishes and tomatoes. Add avocado, salsa verde and lettuce as top layer.

In small bowl mix together sour cream sauce, lime juice, olive oil, garlic powder, basil, salt and pepper. Place the fried tortilla strips on top of the salad. Pour dressing over all, toss gently and serve immediately.

CARNE ASADA SALAD

This salad is another winner. The carne asada (marinated flank or skirt steak) is superb, low in fat and this salad is a perfect way to enjoy the subtle flavor of the meat. The recipe for carne asada is in the Carnitas, Fajitas and Carne Asada Barbecues section of this cookbook. Serves two hungry people for lunch or a light dinner.

1 head lettuce, torn into bite sized pieces
1 tomato, diced
1/2 bunch green onions, chopped
1 cup Mexican cacique, feta or cheddar cheese, grated
1/2 pound carne asada, chilled
1/4 cup salsa fresca
1 1/2 cups tortilla chips

Dressing:
1/3 cup Italian salad dressing
salt and freshly ground pepper to taste

Garnish:
1/2 cup guacamole
1/4 cup thick sour cream sauce (or fat-free sour cream)
2 whole olives

On the bottom of a large salad bowl, layer carne asada, green onions, salsa, and tomatoes. Add grated cheese and lettuce as top layer. Refrigerate up to one hour.

Prior to serving, add salad dressing, salt and pepper. Toss gently. Line two salad plates with tortilla chips. Serve salad onto the plates. Top each serving with half the guacamole mixture and half the sour cream sauce. Place an olive on top of each salad and serve immediately.

GRILLED FAJITAS SALAD

Now here's a new treat with a Wild West - Baja Magic flair — one of those Juan Carlos extravaganzas! (Oh no, not again!) Grilled Fajitas Salad combines the unique flavors of jicama and Mexican pepitas (toasted pumpkin seeds) that are totally Mexican with western hickory-smoked chicken and a few other eclectic treats. Even the dressing, a not-overwhelmingly spicy chile vinaigrette will surprise and delight you.

Nina, another woman friend and I came up with this one. We mixed ingredients from our favorite salads at two different, but equally celebrated restaurants. One is in San Diego. The other is in Cabo San Lucas. Should you wish to tantalize your taste buds by experimenting with ingredients yourself, try using hickory-smoked beef or even broiled shrimp instead of chicken. It will be a highly unforgettable experience no matter which way you prepare it. Just do me one favor. If it's a beautiful, warm day — eat outdoors. Barefoot. With Latin music playing in the background. Serves two hungry people.

Meat:
2 boneless, skinless chicken breasts or 1/2 pound round steak or
1/2 pound deveined shrimp marinated in 1/2 cup hickory marinade

Salad:
1/2 red bell pepper, very thinly sliced and lightly sauteed
1/2 red onion, very thinly sliced and sauteed until wilted
1/2 head romaine, torn into bite size pieces
2 cups field greens (endive, raddiccio and other red leaf lettuces)
1/4 cup very thinly sliced red cabbage
1/2 cup jicama, sliced into thin strips

1 tomato, diced
1/2 cucumber, peeled and diced
1/4 cup roasted pepitas (pumpkin seeds) or sunflower seeds (if unavailable)
1/2 cup queso cacique or feta cheese, crumbled
1 avocado, diced

Dressing:
2 tbsp diced jalapeños (hot) or diced green chiles (mild)
1/4 cup balsamic vinegar
1/4 cup olive oil
1 tsp lime juice
2 tsp garlic powder
1 tsp basil
salt and freshly ground pepper to taste

Marinade chicken, beef or shrimp in hickory marinade for one half hour. Grill, either under the broiler or on the barbecue until done. Slice chicken or beef (not shrimp) into thin strips and chill.

Saute red bell peppers in skillet. Remove and drain. Saute onions. Remove and drain. Place at bottom of large salad bowl. Layer with all other salad ingredients. Chill for up to thirty minutes.

In small bowl, stir together all ingredients for dressing. Pour over salad and toss, adding chicken, beef or shrimp last. Serve immediately on chilled plates.

ALTA CAL'S CAESAR SALAD

(Chicken, Prime Rib or Shrimp)

Recently, every trendy restaurant in Southern California (or upper, if you're from Baja) and even lots of places in both northern and southern Baja have added a Caesar Salad with either prime rib, chicken or shrimp to their luncheon menu. Nina and I have sampled them all over the place and come up with our own, easy-to-make variation. The dressing for this salad is lighter than the traditional Tijuana Caesar Salad and its cheesy, garlicky taste is guaranteed to please you and everyone else you serve it to. It's really good and it's really easy. Serves two

1 head romaine, rinsed and torn into bite-size pieces
2 boneless, skinless pieces of chicken breast, baked 20 minutes and chilled or
1 cup sliced, chilled pieces of left-over prime rib or steak or
1 cup deveined cooked, chilled shrimp
3/4 cups prepared Caesar style croutons
garlic powder to taste
grated Parmesan cheese to taste

Dressing:
1 lemon, halved
Tijuana Caesar Salad dressing or bottled Caesar salad dressing to taste
freshly ground pepper to taste

In large salad bowl, arrange romaine lettuce. Top with chicken, prime rib or shrimp and croutons. Sprinkle with garlic powder and Parmesan cheese. Refrigerate up to one hour.

When ready to serve, squeeze lemon over top of salad. Pour on desired amount of bottled Caesar dressing and toss gently. Serve immediately with garlic bread or hot, buttered tortillas.

ENSALADA PUERTO DE ILUSIÓN

The locals call La Paz, " the port of illusion." On a recent visit there, I asked our waiter at dinner why this was so. His eyes got all misty and dreamy-looking and he gazed out towards the pelicans who were gliding back and forth under the almost surreal lights from the malecón. He sighed as his eyes moved to the line of coconut palms dotting the water's edge. In Spanish he explained to me the mystery and majesty that is La Paz. And it is mysterious and majestic, you know. It just is.

La Paz is more Europe than Mexico to me. It has an understated, adventurous elegance to it — but with just a hint of naughtiness — of that renegade adventurous spirit. Maybe that's because it was originally populated by pirates back in the early days. According to my tourist publications, some of the battles of the Mexican-American War were fought in its streets. These days, it's the capital city of Baja California del Sur, it boasts a population of a quarter of a million and has the highest standard of living in all of Mexico. No kidding! It's

clean, it's cosmopolitan and its economy — which is not based on tourism at all — is flourishing. Folks, La Paz is an amazing place. Go there if you can. It was where Nina and I first discovered Baja Magic back in 1962. And you know, I think that's where Baja Magic was invented. Maybe ....

Nina created with this recipe after dining bayside on the malecón in La Paz that infamous night. This salad is pure Puerto de Illusión. Pure La Paz. It's a true seafood lover's delight, and the moment you take your first bite, you'll be convinced that you're sitting on the malecón under a palapa at the edge of the Sea of Cortez watching the pelicans cruise back and forth in the bay, bathed in the pale glow of the street lights. Be a little bold and serve chilled Pacifico or Corona Beer with this one. Sip it and a balmy, desert breeze will immediately waft its way through your dining room or back yard. You'll hear strains of Mexican music in the distance and whatever stress you've been experiencing will mysteriously vanish. This incredible salad serves two hungry people for lunch or a light dinner.

1 head Romaine, torn into bite
sized pieces
1 tomato, diced
1/2 bunch green onions, chopped
1/2 cup fresh Parmesan cheese,
finely grated
1/2 pound cooked, deveined shrimp,
chilled
1/2 cup shredded carrots
1/4 cup salsa fresca

Dressing:
1/3 cup olive oil
1/4 cup wine vinegar
1 tsp garlic powder
1/4 tsp tarragon
salt and freshly ground pepper to
taste

Garnish:
1/2 cup guacamole
2 whole black olives

On the bottom of a large salad bowl,
layer shrimp, green onions, salsa,
carrots and tomatoes. Add grated
Parmesan and lettuce as top layer.
Refrigerate up to one hour.

Prior to serving, prepare salad
dressing by mixing together salad
dressing, salt and pepper. Pour over
salad and toss gently. Serve salad
on chilled plates and top each serving with half the guacamole mixture.

Place an olive on top of the entire
salad. Serve immediately and enjoy!

CRAB SALAD LORETO

Quick, easy and dyn-o-mite, this
salad is guaranteed to transport
you right to a palapa on the beach,
where you're eating barefoot, with
your feet digging aimlessly in the
grainy sand, sand that's still warm
from the leftover heat of the just-
set-sun. Can you hear the waves quietly lapping against the shore in
front of you as the new moon cuts a
silver sliver in the early evening sky?
Ah yes. Here comes the first star.

You are in Loreto, the oldest permanent settlement in all of Baja. Yes.
It's true. Located nearly three quarters of the way down the peninsula,
on the Sea of Cortez side, Loreto
was founded by Padre Juan María
Salvatierra, a Jesuit priest on
October 25, 1697. The Misión de
Nuestra Señora de Loreto is located
in the center of town. It was the first
of 20 missions founded by Jesuit
priests in Baja before they were

expelled in 1767 for mistreating the Indians. Loreto was the capital of Baja until it was destroyed by a hurricane in 1829 — at which time the capital was moved to La Paz.

So, how are things in Loreto these days? Well, it's been targeted by Fonatur, the Mexican tourist agency, to become the next Cancún or Ixtapa — serious tourist resorts both. It has a lovely malecón, a walkway that runs right along the sea, a new marina and some pretty swanky resorts that offer tennis, golf, fishing and diving. It has daily air service from L.A. And it's growing — both in size and in fame since the big tricentennial fiesta in October of 1997.

So you're ready to go? Me too. Until such time as we get those plane tickets, or have the car packed and ready to roll, we can feed our Baja hunger by cooking up a storm! You'll find the medley of flavors in this tangy crab salad both scrumptious and fame-inspiring. Serves two as a meal.

1 pound cooked crab, diced and chilled
2 avocados, peeled, seeded and diced
1 cup cheddar cheese, shredded

8 - 10 romaine leaves, rinsed and dried
1 1/2 cups tortilla chips

Dressing:
2 tbsp olive oil
2 tbsp Mexican lime juice
1 tsp garlic powder
2 cups salsa fresca

Two to four hours before serving, combine all ingredients except lettuce, crab and chips. Cover and refrigerate. At mealtime, arrange crab mixture on top of lettuce leaves and garnish with chips.

Mix together ingredients for dressing in small bowl. Pour over salad, toss gently and serve.

WILD WEST BARBECUE SALAD

My good friend Kathy is from Oklahoma. Since she's lived by the beach in San Diego and hung out with me for over a decade, she's now officially almost a native. What that means is that she's part cowgirl, part Baja Rat and part pure artist — just like this salad. Interesting and delectable combo, let me assure you. One night when we were in La Bufadora, she was the designated chef for the evening. She made this salad for Nina, me and a bunch of other folks. She used a dry marinade to blacken the chicken, but informed me that London Broil or pork can be spiced up and tenderized with it just as easily. It's easy to do and awesome to eat.

She gave me the recipe, of course. This is a yummy salad that will make you so notorious you'll want to write both me and Kathy thank you notes! (I'm kidding — we both hate writing thank you notes so we certainly don't want you to have to write any to us!) Serves two or three as a meal.

1 large head romaine, rinsed and torn into pieces
1 cup feta cheese, crumbled
2 small Roma tomatoes, diced
1 avocado, sliced
1 cup white corn (you can use frozen)
blue corn tortilla chips
2 breasts chicken, sliced in narrow strips
1 tbsp corn or canola oil

Dry marinade:
1/3 cup American chili powder

Dressing:
1/4 cup olive oil
1/4 cup red wine vinegar
1 tsp oregano
salt and freshly ground pepper to taste.

Layer romaine, cheese, tomatoes, avocado and white corn in a large salad bowl. Place in refrigerator and chill thorougly.

Mix chili powder, sugar and salt together in bowl. Coat the strips of chicken with mixture and fry until done (about 20 minutes) in canola oil. For those of you who want to forego the oil, the chicken breasts can be barbecued before they're sliced instead. After cooking, drain chicken on paper towels and cool slightly.

Add dressing, chicken and blue corn tortilla chips to salad vegetables and toss gently. Serve immediately.

BEANS, RICE & VEGETABLE DISHES

© Bob Bonn 1997

Scaredy Cat

Along with the Mexican staples, refried beans and rice, I'm offering you some new variations of these old standbys. I recommend trying Caribbean Frijoles Negros (black beans) instead of regular frijoles (refried beans) and Sinful Cinnamon Rice. These are new, exciting, even tantalizing side dishes that will guarantee you raised eyebrows and murmurs of approval at your next fiesta.

I've also added some intriguing vegetable dishes to serve with your entrees, such as the Spa Vegetable Kabob and Zucchini with Corn and Peppers. These are zesty, light and delicious. You can alternate these dishes with the salads offered previously to keep your menus fresh and varied; or you can throw a huge fiesta and include something (or lots of things) from each section. Either way, experimentation is fun. It will expand your horizons, enhance your perceptions and raise your consciousness. And it just may inject a little Baja Magic into your life without you even knowing it! Look what happened to Juan Carlos, our notorious margarita-guzzling gato! Why do you think he's hanging out on top of that cardón cactus? Is he afraid of the snake — or has the snake offended him in some way?! Did someone eat too many frijoles?! What do you think?! Want to know what I think? I think that snake is being really parental and lecturing Juan Carlos on the importance of eating his veges. And what's Juan Carlos' response? Well, it's pretty much a, "No way José!" thing. Followed up with a, "Sorry Flaco (Skinny), but you can't make me cuz you can't catch me!" Fade out with that Cheshire grin ....

Wow. Well, for sure there are no canned peas — I promise!

TRADITIONAL FRIJOLES

Refried beans, or frijoles (free-HOE-lays) have been a mainstay in the Mexican diet forever. Served with corn (as in corn tortillas, the two vegetables interact chemically in some miraculous fashion to create a complete protein. That important (to Mexicans) piece of trivia was brought to you by my mother, who swears that the increasing popularity of flour tortillas in the past couple of decades is wreaking havoc on the health of a nation. She refuses to order anything but corn tortillas for that reason. Smart lady, my mom.

Regardless of what you eat with your refried beans, you're going to love them! My family's recipe is guaranteed to taste great even if you opt (as Nina and I do) to take the high road and leave out the bacon grease. My mother tried to leave it out once and caught my dad dumping a huge lump of cold, solidified bacon grease into the bean pot when he thought she was busy folding laundry!

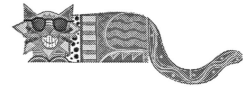

This recipe will make enough beans to feed sixteen to twenty people. I usually make a batch and freeze at least half in smaller amounts to use again and again as a side dish. Also, if you prefer your beans fat-free and in a brothy sauce, try making them Ranchero Style — as explained below.

1 pound package dried pinto beans
4 cups water
1/4 cup bacon grease (optional)
3 tsp garlic powder
2 tbsp chicken bouillon powder
1 tbsp American chili powder

Put beans and water into Dutch oven. Soak at least six hours. Pour beans into colander and rinse thoroughly. Add two cups water back into the Dutch oven, along with bacon grease, garlic powder, bouillon and chili powder. Bring to a boil. Cover and reduce heat, simmering for about four to six hours. Stir occasionally.

You'll know when the frijoles are done because they'll be very tender. If there seems to be too much liquid in the beans, leave the lid off for the last half hour. Stir or mash beans often when lid is off until approximately half of them are mashed and half are still whole.

To prepare Ranchero Style: Leave out the bacon grease. Cook only until beans are barely tender and the mixture has the consistency of bean soup — about two to three hours. You can make part of your batch into refried beans and part into Ranchero style beans. It's up to you!

PAPAS FRITAS CON CHILE VERDE

These potatoes are popular with the people of Baja who do not in any way share our aversion (pretended or otherwise) for fried foods. These are cooked to nearly a crisp with strips of green chile and make an excellent companion for roasted or broiled meats, or even egg dishes at a brunch. Eight servings.

1/2 cup corn or canola oil
2 onions, thinly sliced
2 7 1/2 ounce cans whole green chiles, cut in strips
1 1/2 tsp salt
2 pounds red potatoes, cooked al dente and cubed

In skillet, heat oil to medium heat and fry onions until they are translucent. Add chile strips, potatoes and salt to the onions, and cook, stirring mixture occasionally, for about four minutes, or until potatoes are browned. Serve immediately.

CARIBBEAN FRIJOLES NEGROS

Black beans, cooked in the Caribbean style have become popular in the last decade or so. I first had them in Florida way before that where they'd been introduced by the Cubans. They've since made their way north and west, up the Yucatán peninsula, through mainland Mexico, across the Sea of Cortez and all the way up the Baja Peninsula. Every grocery store I've been into in Baja carries them in cans now, as do our American supermarkets. What are they like? Well, they're more tangy than traditional frijoles and are really great when served with light, tropical fare like some of my eclectic salads and chicken or seafood dishes.

This recipe will make enough beans to feed sixteen to twenty people. I usually make a batch and freeze at least half in smaller amounts to use again and again as a side dish. If, like me and Nina, you prefer to make these without the bacon grease, we both promise you that you won't sacrifice any flavor! And, if you prefer your beans not only fat-free and in a brothy sauce, try making them Ranchero Style — as explained below.

In case this question is rolling around in your mind, let me answer it in advance: Will these beans instantly transport you to the tropics? You bet they will! That's Baja Magic for you — in action!

1 pound package dried black beans
4 cups water
1/4 cup lime juice
1/4 cup bacon grease (optional)
3 tsp garlic powder
2 tbsp chicken bouillon powder
1 - 2 tbsp American chili powder

Put beans and water into Dutch oven. Soak at least six hours. Pour beans into colander and rinse thoroughly. Add two cups water back into the Dutch oven, along with lime juice, bacon grease, garlic powder, bouillon and chili powder. Bring to a boil. Cover and reduce heat, simmering for about four to six hours. Stir occasionally. You'll be able to tell when the frijoles are done because they'll be very tender. If there seems to be too much liquid in the beans, leave the lid off for the last half hour. Stir or mash beans often when lid is off.

To prepare Ranchero Style: Leave out the bacon grease. Cook only until beans are barely tender and the mix-ture has the consistency of bean soup — about two to three hours. You can make part of your batch into refried beans and part into Ranchero style beans. It's up to you!

MEXICAN RICE

This traditional Mexican side dish is super easy to make and always tastes good. I prefer using brown rice because I like it better, but if you don't have any, you can substitute white rice easily. And — if you're really weird, go buy some canned peas and toss a few in. After all — that is what they do in Baja. Right? Right! Serves eight.

3 cups quick brown rice
2 cups water
1 1/2 cups salsa fresca
salt to taste

In medium sized sauce pan bring two cups water and salsa to boil. Add brown rice. Stir well. Cover, reduce heat and simmer for 15 - 20 minutes until fluffy. Add salt to taste. Serve immediately.

WHITE RICE WITH VEGETABLES

This is another uncomplicated recipe that makes a colorful side dish. Light and delicious, it's perfect year- round with any Baja Magic meal. Serves eight.

3 tbsp salad oil
1 onion, chopped
2 cloves garlic, minced
1 1/2 cups uncooked white rice
1/4 tsp cayenne pepper
3 tsp chicken bouillon powder
3 cups boiling water
1 10 ounce package frozen (not canned unless you're a purist, or you're camping) peas, carrots and corn
2 tomatoes, peeled, seeded and chopped

In a large skillet, heat oil over medium heat. Add onion, garlic and rice and cook, stirring constantly until onion is translucent and rice is opaque. In a separate bowl, dissolve the bouillon in boiling water. Stir cayenne into the mixture in skillet. Pour in bouillon/boiling water. Bring to boil, cover and simmer for twenty minutes or until liquid is absorbed. Add peas, carrots, corn and tomatoes. Cook over low heat, stirring until vegetables are heated through, about three minutes.

SPA VEGETABLE KABOBS

My dad's favorite place on Planet Earth is Buena Vista on the East Cape — about 45 minutes north of the Los Cabos Airport. It is a fisherman's paradise, that in the old days (pre-swim-up bar) catered mainly to large groups of loud-mouthed, beer-and-margarita-swilling, poker-playing men and the occasional very adventuresome and equally courageous wife and kids. Needless to say, my family went there — a lot. In those days, the hotel now known as the "Buena Vista Beach Resort" was called "Spa Buena Vista" or just plain old "Spa" to the regulars.

We first had these vegetable kabobs at the Spa about a dozen years and at least as many chefs ago. They're almost identical to grilled vegetables you can get stateside these days, with a couple of small, definitely Baja differences. When you're barbecuing and in the mood for something a bit unconventional, remember these. They take next-to-no-time to make, and are festive, fat free (yeah!) and serve eight.

4 medium zucchini, cut in 1/2 inch chunks
4 yellow squash, cut in 1/2 inch chunks
16 medium sized fresh mushrooms
1/2 to 1 cup salsa fresca
2 tbsp chopped cilantro
8 cherry tomatoes

Microwave or steam zucchini and yellow squash over boiling water for two minutes (until only slightly softened). Skewer zucchini and squash chunks, alternating with mushrooms on skewers. Mix together salsa and cilantro and brush over vegetables. Broil or grill for four minutes, brushing often with salsa. Add a tomato on each skewer and grill two minutes more.

SINFUL CINNAMON RICE

This delectable (practically too-good-too-be-true) rice dish with its unexpected seasonings has its origins somewhere between Cabo San Lucas and Taos, New Mexico (Todos Santos perhaps?!). I'm not sure where it came

from actually. It's just sort of a potpourri of wonderful flavors and textures that's not only pleasing to the eye but a total sensual treat to eat. The combination of long grain rice and vegetables with cinnamon and raisins has created a dramatic side dish that complements any grilled or roasted meat. If you really want to make sure this is a bona fide Baja dish, throw in some canned peas, okay?!

Try it and you'll either find yourself barefoot, in t-shirt and shorts under a palapa in Baja sipping a cerveza with a shot of Hornitos Tequila on the side, (Hornitos is for sipping too — not for shooting) or you might end up sipping a glass of perfectly aged Merlot, inhaling the crisp mountain air of the New Mexico high country as you watch the sun melt into the mountains. Women — turquoise jewelry will drip from your ears, neck and wrists. You'll be wearing a long, colorful skirt, a white blouse and cowboy boots. Men — you're outfitted in jeans, a plaid flannel shirt and a turquoise and silver bolo tie. But be careful. You don't want to spill any red wine on your new clothes!

Which fantasy do you vote for?! Tequila and beer don't stain — in case that impacts your decision! Serves eight.

4 tbsp butter or margarine
1/2 cup carrots, diced
1/2 cup celery, diced
1/2 onion, diced
2 cups long grain rice
1/2 tsp salt
1 tbsp ground cinnamon
1/2 cup raisins
6 cups water

Melt two tablespoons butter in deep saucepan over medium heat. Reduce heat, add carrots, celery and onion and cook, covered for ten minutes. Stir occasionally. Add rice, salt, cinnamon, raisins and water to pan and bring to boil over high heat. When the water has reduced to the level of the rice, lower heat, cover and cook 15 to 20 minutes, stirring occasionally. Just prior to serving, add remaining butter.

CHILI ONION RINGS

Chili onion rings are a renowned, spicy Baja treat that can be served harmoniously with grilled meat, fish or chicken. So simple and yet so very tasty! Oh yes! Serves six to eight.

2 large yellow onions, thinly sliced
3 cups flour
1 tbsp cayenne pepper
1 tbsp American chili powder

1 tbsp paprika
salt and pepper to taste
5 cups corn oil

Separate onions into rings. Mix flour, cayenne, chili powder, paprika, salt and pepper in a bowl. Heat the oil in a deep fryer or heavy skillet until a drop of water sizzles when put into the oil. Dredge some of the onion rings in flour mixture and fry until golden. Drain on paper towels, keeping them warm while frying the remaining rings. Don't dredge the onions until just prior to frying or they'll give off too much moisture. Serve immediately.

ZUCCHINI WITH CORN AND PEPPERS

A colorful addition to any meal, these lightly fried red, green and yellow vegetables are delicately flavored with garlic. A long-time favorite of my mother's, their freshness and zip makes them appealing to both party crowds or family groups. And of course, they're an excellent way to use up those overflowing, overwhelming quantities of zucchini you may have gotten stuck with this summer! Serves eight.

1 1/2 tbsp margarine
2 1/2 pounds zucchini, cut into 1/2 inch cubes
1 1/2 cups corn cut from four ears
1/2 red bell pepper, seeded and chopped
1/2 green bell pepper, seeded and chopped
1 onion, chopped
3 cloves garlic, minced
salt and pepper to taste

In large skillet, melt margarine over high heat. Add zucchini, corn, bell peppers, onion and garlic. Cook, stirring frequently until most of vegetable liquid has evaporated and vegetables are tender-crisp. Serve immediately.

CHEF CARLOS LEYVA VALDEZ' RAJAS EN CREMA

Here's an interesting piece of trivia for you. In Mexico, everyone has two last names. The first one, in this case, Leyva, is the last name of Carlos' father. The second one, Valdez, is his mother's last name. How often do well-meaning (but ignorant) gringos call a Mexican by the wrong last name?! I hate to tell you, but we do it all the time! The correct last name is the middle one. Here in U.S., when a wife uses her maiden name as her middle name, as in Nina Hazard Baldwin — it's totally different. It's just one of those cultural enigmas — like driving on the left side of the road in Britain — that takes a little getting used to!

On a recent visit to the newly rechristened "Buena Vista Beach Resort," Chef Carlos Leyva gave me the following recipe to include in this book. If you're ever in the East Cape, do stop by for a visit. My dad swears that his buddy, Chuy Valdez, runs the best hotel around — and has the finest fishing boats with the greatest captains. It's an excellent place to hang out, even for people like me who don't fish or dive. I do kayak, I do snorkel, I do swim, I do play water volleyball, I do beachwalk and I do climb hills at sunrise — and I definitely do hang out — either in my room-side hammock or at the swim-up bar.

Try this recipe. It is divine and goes beautifully with any chicken, beef or seafood dish. Serves four.

4 fresh chiles — either poblanos, pasillas or Anaheim (or substitute 1 7 ounce can whole green chiles)
1 large onion, sliced

4 tbsp butter
2 cups Nestlé Media Crema (found in Baja) or thin sour cream sauce (from Salsa section)
1/2 tsp salt (or to taste)
1 cup grated Chihuahua or Asadero cheese (Jack or Feta can be substituted)

If using fresh chiles — in large skillet, cook chiles over hot flame until they become blistered and blackened. Remove from heat and put in a plastic bag with a tablespoon or so of water to steam them. Wait five minutes, then rinse the chiles, peeling off the skin. Slice chiles into strips and set aside. (If using canned chiles, rinse, slice into strips and set aside.)

Melt butter in skillet. Add onion and cook until translucent. Add chiles, salt and crema or light sour cream sauce. Stir until heated clear through. Remove from heat and serve immediately, garnishing with grated cheese.

TORTILLAS, BREADS & BURGERS

Love on the Ranch

Mexicans have traditionally used corn and flour tortillas as the starch staple in their diets, so they don't bake many breads. A trip to any panadería (pahn-ah-der-EE-yah — bakery) in Baja will show you, however, that fresh baked bolillos (boe-LEE-yoes — Mexican hard rolls) are a favorite of theirs.

When I was a kid, my mom would insist that we stop at the panadería before we got to our destination. If we got there early enough in the morning, Nina and I would sneak out back behind the bakery and watch the baker slide huge trays of hot, fresh rolls out of the rounded, Indian-style outdoor brick ovens. Out with the bolillos — in with trays of dough. Our well-rehearsed, endearing smiles were intended to net us each a roll straight from the oven. And, to our parents' chagrin, we were usually successful.

Oh, how my mouth waters at the memory of biting into a piping hot bolillo. They're still baked twice a day in Baja, first thing in the morning and during the siesta period right after the mid-day meal. Although the Mexican bakeries specialize more in sweet breads, donuts and cookies these days, bolillos can still be bought for 10 to 15 cents each. Their coarse texture comes from unbleached flour and their flavor is rich and earthy — a true peasant bread bursting with Baja Magic. And you'll rarely find them in the U.S.A. Then there are those Mexican cookies, and donuts and pastries and — all so good and so totally different than anything you'd buy in a gringo bakery. You just have to go see for yourself. There's no way around it!

My first taste of a just-made corn tortilla was at Kilometer 181, about 120 miles south of Ensenada, back in the mid-sixties. We were the only campers on a beach that went on forever. In fact, the only other people we saw all week were an old rancher and his wife, María. They invited us to their home — a tiny two room structure built entirely from scraps of plywood, tar paper and other materials scavenged from who-knows-where. Mexican ingenuity to the "T." María patted tiny balls of maza into skinny pancakes, tossed them onto the split oil drum that served as her stove, browned them on both sides, flipped them off the grill and handed me one filled with beans and stewed beef. Oh — was it ever good!

If you're curious about where to get the freshest tortillas in Baja nowadays, don't go looking for them in a panadería. You can buy them hot off the press (the lumps of dough are actually pressed and cooked by machine right in front of your eyes) in supermarkets like Gigante or Calimax or in a specialty store known as a tortilleria (tor-tee-yer-EE-uh).

To round out this section, I've added a camping favorite of my family's to the bread recipes here, Jalapeño Corn Bread. It's different from its Southern (as in south of the Mason-Dixon Line) cousin in that it's flavored with jalapeño chiles, whole kernel corn and lots of cheese. It's great when you're eating barefoot out under the Baja stars, warming your toes at the campfire — and it's great at home, sitting cross-legged on the living room carpet with a fire blazing in the fireplace. Its uniquely Baja flavor is truly delicious! And then, of course, there's that staple of every expatriate's diet, the Baja Beach Burger. Gotta try one of those!

CORN TORTILLAS

Do you recall that corn tortillas comprise half of that complete protein my mother always bragged about? (Right — the other half is beans — very good!)

Should you get hit over the head with the urge to make your own corn tortillas, here is the recipe. Most people, and I'll confess I'm one of those, find it easier to buy fresh or frozen tortillas in the grocery store. But these are fun to make at least once, and if you have kids, they make a great project for a rainy day. Makes a dozen.

2 cups maza de harina (dehydrated maza flour)
1 1/4 to 1 1/3 cups water

Mix maza with enough warm water to make dough hold together. Using your hands, shape dough into smooth ball. Divide into 12 equal pieces and roll into balls, flattening each slightly. Using two cloths that have been dipped in water and wrung dry, place each ball between the cloths. Roll with light, even strokes until tortilla is about six inches in diameter. Carefully pull back cloths, trim tortilla to a round shape and place it on a square of wax paper. Repeat, stacking between pieces of wax paper.

Peel off top piece of wax paper. Turn tortilla, paper side up, onto a preheated, ungreased skillet over medium high heat. As tortilla warms, peel off remaining wax paper. Cook for 1 1/2 to 2 minutes, turning frequently until tortilla is soft but flecked with brown specks. Serve immediately, or store in refrigerator or freezer. Makes 12.

FLOUR TORTILLAS

Here is the ambitious, adventurous cook's recipe for flour tortillas. Makes 12 nine inch tortillas. This recipe also forms the basis for those killer Special Quesadillas (see Appetizer section).

3 cups self-rising flour
1 tsp salt
2 tbsp solid vegetable shortening (or lard if you're into authenticity)
1 1/8 cups water

In large bowl, cut shortening into flour. Add salt. Stir water in slowly with a fork until a large ball of dough is formed. Cover and let sit for 20 minutes. Turn out onto a board and knead until smooth. Divide into 12 pieces and shape each into a smooth ball. Flatten each ball into a four or five inch patty, then roll into a nine-inch round.

After each tortilla is rolled out, place it on a preheated, ungreased skillet over medium high heat. When blisters appear on tortilla, flatten immediately with wide spatula. Turn tortilla often until blisters turn a light brown. Serve immediately or store in refrigerator or freezer. Makes a dozen.

JALAPEÑO CORN BREAD

Jalapeño chiles, real corn and lots of cheese distinguishes this corn bread from the old-fashioned, all-American ya'all version of corn bread. It's not too fiery, but makes an awesome side dish for roasted or grilled foods. I love it! My mom used to serve it with fresh fried chicken (fresh because the chickens were purchased — very recently alive — from rancheros we happened to come upon in our travels up and down the dusty back roads of Baja) during our summer camping trips on the Pacific side of the peninsula back when I was in high school! Mom tried to get away with only putting a couple of jalapeños in the batter, but Nina, our dad and I had a conspiracy going. As soon as she left the camper, even if the corn bread was already in the oven, we'd sneak it out and add a whole bunch more diced chiles! You can just imagine her shock when she took her first bite of what she thought was a subtly-flavored, lightly spiced delicacy! The look on her face, the way she rushed for a soda and gulped it down — these are priceless memories! Truly they are. Serves 12.

2 - 10 jalapeño chiles, finely chopped with seeds
1 3 1/2 ounce can diced green chiles
1 onion, finely diced
1 17 ounce can creamed corn
1/2 tsp baking soda
1/2 tsp salt
1 tbsp sugar
2 eggs
3/4 cup buttermilk
1/3 cup corn or canola oil
1 cup cheddar cheese, grated
2 cups yellow corn meal

Preheat oven to 350 degrees. Grease a 9 x 14 inch pan. In a large bowl, mix jalapeños with corn and onion. Beat in baking soda, salt and sugar, then add the eggs one at a time, beating well. Add buttermilk and oil, then cheese and cornmeal.

Pour batter into pan and bake for 30 to 40 minutes, or until the top is brown and a toothpick inserted in the center comes out clean. Cool in pan and serve in squares.

BOLILLOS (MEXICAN HARD ROLLS)

Bolillos are different than French rolls or other hard rolls. The crust is crisp, but the roll is soft and almost crumbly inside. The texture is coarse and the flavor is uniquely Mexican. These rolls are great when toasted and served with butter and jam for breakfast. Or, split them in half and use them to make Baja style "tortas," or sandwiches, much like torpedoes. Put anything you want inside — from taco and burrito stuffings to tuna salad for a truly memorable Baja Magic sandwich (or buy them at any roadside torta stand in every Baja town). And bolillos are wonderful served piping hot at dinner. Just split them in half and load the insides up with butter or roasted garlic. Then wrap them in a cloth and place in a festive basket.

As I mentioned in the introduction to this section, in Mexican panaderías you can buy bolillos fresh twice a day, for 10 to 15 cents apiece. Today the peasant bread is losing its authenticity and becoming more Americanized as the bakers use more refined flour. If you want yours to taste really authentic, try buying unrefined flour from a health food store. Makes 12 scrumptious rolls.

2 cups water
1 1/2 tbsp sugar
1 tbsp salt
2 tbsp butter or margarine
1 pkg active dry yeast
6 cups unsifted flour
1 tbsp corn oil
1 tbsp cornstarch dissolved in 1/2 cup water

In saucepan combine water, sugar, salt and butter. Heat over low heat, stirring until just barely boiling. Pour into large mixing bowl, add yeast and stir until dissolved. With an electric mixer, beat in five cups flour to form a dough ball.

Turn dough onto a board coated with about 1/2 cup flour and knead for 10 minutes. Dough should feel velvety. Add more flour if necessary to prevent dough from sticking to board. Form into a ball and place in an oiled bowl.

Turn dough over so that all sides are oiled. Cover with plastic wrap and let rise in a warm place until dough has doubled in size (about 1 1/2 hours). Punch dough to release air bubbles, then turn out onto lightly floured board.

Divide into twelve equal pieces. Form each piece into a smooth ball. Shape each into an oblong by rolling it and gently pulling from the center to the ends until the ball is about four inches long and center is thicker than ends.

Place rolls about two inches apart on greased baking sheets, cover lightly with a towel and let rise for 30 minutes or until they've doubled in size. In small saucepan, heat cornstarch and water to boiling. Cool slightly and then brush each roll with cornstarch mixture. Using a sharp knife, cut a slash 3/4 inch deep and 2 inches long on top of each roll. Bake at 375 degrees for 35 to 40 minutes, until rolls are golden brown and sound hollow when tapped. Cool and wrap tightly to store.

BAJA BEACH BURGERS

In case you don't know this, the Sea of Cortez does not boast the hot wave action that the Pacific side of the peninsula does. While it can get really windy and the seas can get plenty rough on the east coast of Baja, the water overall is not only much warmer, but much calmer. One can barely body

Summer Fun

© Bob Bonn 1997

Cat Fishing

surf there, much less wield a surf-board successfully. So — when I first heard there was a decent surfing beach in Los Cabos, I was more than skeptical. I didn't believe it at all. I thought this person's synapses were misfiring and that he'd gotten himself more than a little confused — enough to mistake, say the big waves at Todos Santos for the belly busters on the East Cape. Then he took me there and I saw that he was right on. I was the one who was mistaken!

The beach is located on the south end of San Jose del Cabo, just to the north of the elegant Palmilla resort and the day I was there, the break even at mid-day was perfect — the water light green and glassy — the waves close to six feet. There were plenty of surfers out there too, and even a couple of boogy boarders and body surfers. The 86 degree water made wet suits unnecessary, to be stored in the surfers' VW vans and saved for the colder waters on the west coast.

We had lunch at Zipper's that day — a famous meeting, greeting and eating place for the surf set. It's situated right smack in the middle of their beach, after all. The menu there was gringo all the way and everyone in my group ordered Cheeseburgers! Naturally, being Parrot Headed Jimmy Buffett fans for over 20 years, Nina and I did not fail to make the connec-tion between his famous ballad, "Cheeseburger in Paradise" and our current situation. As we reflected on our lunch, this beach, Jimmy's song and the abundance of hamburger and cheeseburger-serving restaurants all over Baja, we realized that our cook-book wouldn't be complete without a cheeseburger recipe. Because, if you've been out of the U.S. for any length of time, you'll discover, like all expatriated Americans do, that the one food you crave the most is — yeah, you got it — a cheeseburger!

This is our dad's camping version of the Baja Beach Burger. We recom-mend serving them with Teaque Slaw, Papas Fritas con Chile Verde and a frosty Pacifico or Coke. Serves six.

Burgers:
2 lb lean ground beef
1 cup white onions, minced
2 tsp cumin, powdered
1 tsp garlic powder
1 tsp salt
1/2 tsp pepper
1 egg
6 hamburger buns
6 slices cheese (be as creative as you want here)

Trimmings:
lettuce
sliced tomatoes
sliced dill pickles
sliced red or white onions
mayonnaise, mustard and catsup

In large bowl, mix first seven ingredients. Form into six patties and grill on the barbecue for approximately five minutes on each side. During the last minute, top each burger with a slice of cheese. Arrange the buns around the edges of the grill to lightly toast. Then slap a burger onto each bun, let everyone load theirs up with their favorite toppings and dig in!

FULL-ON FIESTA FARE:

CARNITAS, FAJITAS & CARNE ASADA

Mariachi Cactus

Welcome to Party Central. That describes this section of Cooking With Baja Magic. Any of these recipes can serve as the focal point of a casual family dinner or a grand fiesta. Try one. Try two. Try them all! You'll be serving up "the best in good time cooking from both sides of the border." Guaranteed. Ask your guests to dress for the occasion — you know — colorful flowing skirts and peasant blouses for the women. For the men, suggest Hawaiian shirts and shorts with flip flops if it's summertime. They ought to be able to handle that! If the weather's cold, then jeans and sweaters will do. If people want to give themselves a Southwest touch, by all means encourage the Indian silver jewelry, the hand-woven fabrics, the bolo ties.

And oh — if you line the walkway to your front door with luminarios, which are brown paper sacks filled with sand, each with a candle inside you'll have your guests almost all the way "in the mood" before they even ring your doorbell. Then, add some festive paper plates with matching napkins, some fresh (or colorful paper) flowers and lots of the right kind of music (ask at the Latin American section of your local music store) — you'll have everybody just oozing Baja Magic even before they pop the top off their first cerveza!

Carnitas, Fajitas and Carne Asada are foods that have become popular north of the border in the last two decades. But before that, the only place in California that anyone had ever heard of carne asada (which is marinated strips of flank or skirt steak that are grilled to perfection over charcoal) was in the Imperial Valley, about 100 miles due east of San Diego and only a few miles north of Mexicali. That was then. This is now — and now every taco shop, Mexican restaurant and Southwestern eatery serves a variation of it. But it started in Baja and if you ask me, it tastes better when I eat it in Mexico than it ever does up here. Do you think I'm imagining things? Most likely. I think I'd just rather be in Baja most of the time!

Like Carne Asada, Fajitas have become so popular in this region that even fast food chains like McDonald's and Jack in the Box serve them. (Oh dear!) They're made by marinating chicken, beef or shrimp with chiles and vegetables in oil, vinegar and spices and then stir frying them. Made into burritos and served with condiments, fajitas can be quite a feast. Rumor has it they really originated somewhere on the Texas - Mexico border, in the lowlands around the Rio Grande. But then I've heard other rumors from one or two restaurant owners in Rosarito Beach and Ensenada that they (or their relatives anyway) dreamed up Fajitas. Who knows?! For the sake of this cookbook, how about if we just go along with the second story?!

Carnitas, which originated in the Tampico section of Mexico (I know this for a fact!) are becoming increasingly fashionable as well. I don't deep fry the pork (like the Mexicans do) when I make my carnitas. I buy almost the leanest pork roast I can find (the no-fat kind turns out too dry) then bake it in salsa and spices for several hours until it's fork tender. I love, love, love Carnitas! So will you, even if, unlike the magazine ads, you still don't think of pork as "the other white meat!" You just may be converted by Carnitas. In fact, I'd bet money on it.

If you're feeling tentative about throwing a fiesta — hey — that's okay. Close your eyes. Take a deep breath. Smell that salty ocean breeze. Listen to the sea gulls shrieking overhead. Exhale. Breathe in again — this time inhaling some of that Baja Magic. Now you're ready to crank yourself up and get into party gear. Go for it!

Ready? Good. I see you. You're already in your car, on the way to the grocery store with your fiesta shopping list in hand and a Jimmy Buffett tune blaring out of your tape player! All right!

CARNITAS

I love to cook carnitas for any sized crowd. It's requires little preparation time, which is a big plus and actually, I'd have to say it's Nina and my favorite birthday party fare. The pork is tangy, crispy but not greasy (the way I do it) and makes a terrific fiesta dish. As a buffet, serve a platter of steaming carnitas with corn and flour tortillas, and have your guests make their own burritos filled with the succulent pork and the condiments listed below. On the side, serve a fruit or vegetable salad. This recipe for carnitas serves eight to ten. And it's to die for!

1 4 - 5 pound lean boneless pork loin roast, with excess fat removed
1 cup salsa verde
1 large onion, minced
4 cloves garlic, minced
1 tbsp seasoned salt
2 tsp pepper

On the side, buffet style:
2 dozen warm corn and/or flour tortillas
1 cup frijoles negros
1 cup thick sour cream sauce
1 can sliced olives (optional)
2 cups Chihuahua or Jack cheese, grated
1 bunch green onions, chopped
2 avocados, sliced and sprinkled with lime juice
1 bunch cilantro, stems removed and diced

2 bunches of whole radishes, stems removed
1 cup salsa fresca
1 cup salsa verde

Place pork roast in 9 x 14 pan. Rub garlic into the roast. Sprinkle with salt and pepper. Cover with salsa verde and onions. Loosely cover the pan with aluminum foil. Bake at 300 degrees for four and a half hours, or until fork tender.

Remove roast from oven. Cool until you can touch the meat comfortably. Remove from pan and place on cutting board. Skim fat off pan juices. Using two forks, shred the pork. Remove fat from meat. When all meat is shredded, return it to the pan and mix the pan juices thoroughly into the pork.

Return to oven. Cook, uncovered for 30 minutes or until pork is crispy on top. Remove from oven. Turn pork. Return to oven and cook another 20 minutes, until pork is crispy on top and there is almost no liquid left in the pan. Serve as suggested above.

FAJITAS: CHICKEN, BEEF or SHRIMP
LA CONCHA BEACH CLUB STYLE

Fajitas have been the rage throughout the Southwest and Baja for several years now. This recipe came came to us courtesy of our waiter at the La Concha Beach Club, which is right to the north of the famed Melia Cabo Real resort in Los Cabos. It's home to a gigantic tide pool — a naturally occurring salt water formation big enough for plenty of people to swim in, with enough room for us to dive off the rocks and play in the waves, enough room even for us to frolic with the pelicans who were doing just about the same thing we were. With the sole exception that they were scouting out their lunch and dive-bombing into the water to get it. We swam first and then went up the cliff to the restaurant and ate sizzling hot fajitas on the terrace under a giant palapa. And soaked up the incomparable beauty of the place!

Fajitas are incredibly simple to prepare, they're fun to eat and they're delicious. These make enough great eats and good times for eight people. Ole! Ole! Ole! Mariachi music or salsa music from Texas is definitely in order to set the right mood for a Fajitas Fiesta. And maybe barefoot would be good too...

3 pounds boneless chicken breasts, cut into chunks -or- 3 pounds round steak, cut into
 chunks or 3 pounds large shrimp, deveined
3 green bell peppers, cut into chunks
3 yellow bell peppers, cut into chunks
3 red bell peppers, cut into chunks
1 1/2 large onions, diced
2 tomatoes, cut into chunks
1/4 to 3/4 cup sliced jalapeños (hot) or 1 3 1/2 ounce can diced green chiles (milder)
3/4 cup olive oil
1/2 cup Mexican lime juice
4 tbsp wine vinegar
2 tbsp oregano
1 tsp Worcestershire Sauce
 cup beer
3 tbsp garlic powder
salt and pepper to taste

On the side, buffet style:
2 dozen corn or flour tortillas
2 cups guacamole
2 cups salsa fresca
1 cup thick sour cream sauce

In large bowl combine chicken, steak or shrimp with red and green bell peppers, onion, tomatoes, and jalapeños or green chiles.

In small bowl mix together oil, lime juice, beer, garlic, Worcestershire, vinegar, oregano, salt and pepper. Pour over meat and vegetable mixture and toss gently. Cover. Marinate three hours or overnight in refrigerator. About twenty minutes before dinner is to be served, heat a large skillet or wok until very, very hot. Drain off excess marinade. Pour chicken, steak or shrimp mixture into skillet and stir fry for six to eight minutes, until done.

Place in serving dish. Put serving dish on electric or Sterno hot plate so that when it's served at the table, it stays hot. Put a bowl of guacamole, a bowl of salsa and a bowl of sour cream sauce on the table. Wrap tortillas in foil and heat in oven, or cook in microwave until steaming. Serve in a bread basket to keep warm. Have each guest put fajita mixture into a tortilla. Garnish with guacamole, salsa and sour cream. Roll up into a burrito.

CARNE ASADA

When I lived in the Imperial Valley in the mid 70's, Carne Asada was unheard of anywhere else in the U.S.A. You could buy it, marinated and ready to throw on the grill at every independent, Mom and Pop market in the valley. Everyone in the farming community of El Centro (where I lived) had their favorite "source" for the lean, flavorful flank steak. That hasn't changed. El Centro-ites still barbecue carne asada at every opportunity. But — its fame has spred considerably in the last couple of decades.

When I moved away, I discovered that I had become quite attached (addicted perhaps?!) to Carne Asada. I loved the whole ritual that surrounded it, from the trip to the Mexican meat market for the best meat available to the chopping of goodies for salsa together with the other women in the kitchen and the making of the guacamole to the sound of the meat sizzling on the barbecue. I loved hanging out with my friends and shooting the breeze, inhaling the aroma of the meat as our stomachs' growled in time with the beat of the music. I missed the mad rush for the serving table when the meat was finally ready. To this day, I never fail to smile at the memories of

the empty tortillas being transformed into bulging burritos, smothered in fresh salsa in a matter of moments. Then, silence would descend on the party (except for the music of course) while everyone practically inhaled their burritos. We would stuff ourselves until we were groaning — but no one ever seemed to stop eating until everything was gone. It was that good. Really, it was. It wasn't just a barbecue — it was an event — a celebration!

I longed to recreate that wonderful, intimate yet lively feeling I got from those Carne Asada Barbecues in El Centro, so I decided to start with the meat. I started experimenting with marinades until I came up with my own recipe. I stuck with it for years, but I wasn't ever happy with it — it just wasn't quite right. So I cheated. I asked my friend, Leslie to help me get it right, and she did. The recipe she gave me is a hybrid between two of El Centro's most famous meat markets. At long last I have the real thing — and now — so can you!

As you prepare your own Carne Asada Fiesta, don't forget to serve up some delectable Baja appetizers. Pass around a pitcher of Margaritas, Sangría or just leave an ice chest full of (Mexican) beer out in the back yard and let people help themselves. Put on some really good mariachi or salsa music and watch as everyone starts tapping their feet in time with the beat. Check out their noses as they turn and inhale those awesome Carne Asada fumes. Then, finally, when all is ready, send your guests over to the buffet table. Let them whip together their own tacos and burritos by filling tortillas with chunks of carne asada and the other condiments listed below. On the side, serve a Watermelon Fruit Salad.

Don't forget to set a colorful table and remember that mood music! It's a must! I promise you, your backyard barbecue will take on the lively air of a full-on Baja Blast. Serves six.

3 pounds flank or round steak, tenderized and sliced very thin
1/3 cup fresh lemon or Mexican lime juice
1 large white onion, thinly sliced

3 tbsp garlic powder
2 tbsp oregano
seasoned salt to taste
pepper to taste

On the side, buffet style:
2 dozen corn and flour tortillas
1 cup frijoles
1 cup thick sour cream sauce
1 can sliced olives (optional)
2 cups Chihuahua or Jack cheese, grated
1 bunch green onions, chopped
2 avocados, sliced and sprinkled with lime juice
1 bunch cilantro, stems removed and diced
1 cup salsa fresca and/or salsa verde

Place the steak in one or two 9 x 14 pans. Sprinkle the seasoned alt, pepper, oregano and garlic evenly over the meat. Pour lemon or lime juice over everything. Top with sliced onions. Seal the pan with plastic wrap and leave in the refrigerator for one to two days to marinate. When ready, remove meat from marinade and cook on a very hot barbecue until cooked to desired doneness. Remove from grill, slice into thin strips and serve immediately, as suggested above.

B.A.J.A

M.A.G.I.C

TACOS, BURRITOS & TOSTADAS

Five for Dinner

Tacos, burritos and tostadas — the indispensable, traditional Mexican foods that everyone in the United States is familiar with — thanks to Taco Bell! Although I like Taco Bell (and I love their hot sauce!), don't expect the recipes here to bear much resemblance to the food they sell. Theirs may taste good, but it's hardly authentic Baja cuisine! The minute I cross the border and head south, visions of street tcos start dancing in my head. Street tacos? Are you asking yourself, "What in the world are street tacos?!" Well, I'll let you in on a secret. They are the best! I could eat Mexican street tacos at least every other day. But, you ask — aren't they just loaded with those toxic amoebas? Not to the best of my knowledge.

Okay. Imagine this if you will — you're walking down the street in Tijuana, Rosarito or Ensenada (border tourist towns, all) and you smell that distinctive aroma that tells you someone nearby is barbecuing steak. Your olfactories are instantly electrified, your mouth waters and you turn your head to see where the wondrous smell is coming from. Two stores away is an outdoor counter jammed with people sitting on stools, hunched over plates of food.

You move in for a closer look. They're scarfing plates full of tacos. The lady behind the counter tosses a few slabs of carne asada onto a grill behind the counter, cooks them, removes the meat to a wooden board and quickly chops it into tiny pieces with a meat cleaver. Meanwhile, she's heated up corn tortillas and she heaps grilled meat on top of each tortilla. She hands a plate to a salivating gringo and motions for him to add cilantro, roasted chiles, cheese, onions, tomatoes, any of several types of salsa, cabbage, huge radishes and sour cream sauce to his tacos. He reaches out and piles on the goodies.

You see a couple paying their bill (la cuenta). They start to get up. Before they're all the way off their stools, you and your companion have slid onto them. You're ready. Order up. And don't forget an ice cold, frosty bottle of Coca Cola or a cerveza. Hey, wait. I want to be in this picture too. Paint me in, will you? My taste buds are all revved up and ready. Let's let's go eat tacos ....

 Both Baja and U.S.A. Californians have gotten pretty creative with our tacos, burritos and tostadas. (You can also order burritos and tostadas at these sidewalk taco bars.) You aren't limited to just carne asada, but can often order shredded beef, carnitas and turkey, lamb, fish and ceviche. I even had lobster tacos once for lunch at the Bay of L.A. The recipes for all of them are here, except the carne asada, which you already have.

To start with, I've provided you instructions for how to make tacos, burritos and tostadas. Then I've given you the recipes for a variety of fillings. If you have left-over meat (like duck or lamb) and get the urge to make up your own variation of tacos, burritos or tostadas, go for it! That, my friend, shows you have caught the Baja Magic attitude. And remember, if you ever find yourself standing in front of a street taco stand — don't be a coward. Let your renegade spirit loose. Indulge yourself. Try those street tacos! You'll never regret it!

HOW TO MAKE TACOS

It seems like tacos are everyone's first introduction to Mexican food. Initially, the only kind of tacos around were made from ground beef. (Boring!) Now there is a myriad of meat, poultry and seafood fillings for tacos, all of which follow in this section.

I've also listed two ways to serve tacos: using fried tortilla shells or hot, soft tortillas. You're probably more familiar with fried tacos, but as you read on the previous page, soft tacos are served curbside all over Baja and mainland Mexico. Aside from being authentic, they're lower in fat and calories. They taste just as good, though and are actually preferable if you're making fish, carne asada or carnitas tacos. The recipe below serves four to six.

2 cups shredded beef or other filling (all recipes for fillings follow)
12 corn tortillas
1/2 cup corn or canola oil (optional - soft tacos aren't fried)
2 cups Chihuahua or Jack cheese, grated
1 tomato, diced
1 bunch green onions, chopped
1/2 head lettuce or cabbage, shredded
1 cup salsa fresca and/or salsa verde

FRIED TACOS:

In small frying pan, heat oil until a drop of water sizzles immediately when added to it. Fry tortilla lightly on one side. Turn and fry lightly on the other side. Before tortilla becomes crisp, bend it in half, using tongs and a fork to hold it steady and crisp the folded end. Remove from oil and drain on paper towel. Repeat with all 12 tortillas.

Heat filling until steaming. Place one to two tablespoons filling mixture inside taco shell. Add shredded lettuce, onions, tomatoes and top with cheese. Repeat for all tacos. Serve immediately.

STREET TACOS (SOFT TACOS):
The difference here is that soft tacos are not fried. Heat tortillas in the oven or microwave until hot and pliable. Fold and fill in the same way as fried tacos. If your tacos seem inclined to fall apart, try using two tortillas for double the strength. Serve immediately. Soft tacos are served street side in Baja. I include corn tortillas, along with flour tortillas at all fiestas where people build their own tacos and burritos. (See previous section on Carnitas, Fajitas and Carne Asada Barbecues.)

QUESA-TACOS (A BAJA STREET TACO EXTRAVAGANZA):

One of my all-time favorite tacos are carne asada quesa-tacos. The only difference between soft street tacos and these are that after you fill the corn tortilla with meat, you add some grated Jack cheese and flip it back onto the grill (or frying pan) until the cheese is melted. Then add the rest of the goodies. It is beyond delicious!

HOW TO MAKE BURRITOS

As I described in the section on Full-On Fiesta Fare, burritos make a wonderful do-it-yourself buffet dinner. They're like street tacos, only they're made with flour tortillas and are twice as big as corn tortillas — which means you can cram a lot more goodies into them!

The flour tortillas are put on the table in a covered dish, the meat or fish is put in another serving dish and all other fillings, such as those listed below are displayed, along with a variety of salsas. People put whatever ingredients they choose into their burrito, roll it up and eat it. It's easy for the chef and entertaining for the guests.

2 cups shredded beef or other filling (all filling recipes follow)
8 large flour tortillas
1 cup refried beans (optional)

1 cup thick sour cream sauce (optional)
1 can sliced olives (optional)
1 cup guacamole (optional)
2 cups Chihuahua or Jack cheese, grated
1 bunch green onions, chopped
1 bunch cilantro, stems removed and diced
1 cup salsa fresca and/or salsa verde
1 12 ounce can enchilada sauce or 1 1/2 cups Salsa Ranchera (optional — from Salsa section)

Heat tortillas in oven or microwave until hot and pliable. Heat filling in small saucepan or microwave until steaming. Fill with meat, beans, sour cream, olives, guacamole, cheese and onions. (Note that many of these items are optional. You can use all or only a few as your mood suits you.)

Fold one end and roll into a log-like shape. If you prefer sauce over your burrito, immediately prior to serving, pour heated enchilada sauce over burritos and top with cheese. Heat in oven or microwave until cheese is melted, if desired.

HOW TO MAKE TOSTADAS

Tostadas are like flat tacos that usually have a layer of frijoles on the bottom and different fillings, lettuce, guacamole, cheese and salsa on top. Tostadas are almost-salads and are perfect for a light meal. They too make great buffet fare. The recipe below serves six.

2 cups shredded beef or other filling (all filling recipes follow)
12 corn tortillas
1/2 cup corn or canola oil
1 1/2 cups frijoles (optional)
1 tomato, diced
1 bunch green onions, chopped
1/2 head lettuce, shredded
2 cups guacamole
2 cups Chihuahua or Jack cheese, grated
1 cup salsa fresca and/or salsa verde

In small frying pan, heat oil until a drop of water sizzles immediately when added to it. Fry tortilla lightly on one side. Turn and fry lightly on the other side. Remove from oil and drain on paper towel. Repeat with all 12 tortillas.

Heat filling and frijoles until steaming. Place one to two tablespoons of frijoles on top of fried tortilla. Top with another two tablespoons of filling. Add shredded lettuce, onions, tomatoes and guacamole. Top with cheese. Repeat for all tostadas. Serve immediately. And enjoy.

SHREDDED BEEF FILLING for TACOS, BURRITOS & TOSTADAS

There are two ways to make shredded beef. The lightening-fast way uses canned roast beef, while the traditional way takes hours. Whether you're a purist and take the longer pot roast route, or if you're a hurried cook or short-cut seeking camper (like me most of the time) and opt for the quick way — your beef will end up savory, tender and delicious! And no one will ever know if you cheat (unless you confess, of course).

THE CHEATER'S SUPER EASY SHREDDED BEEF:

1 12 ounce can roast beef in gravy, rinsed
1/2 cup salsa fresca
salt and pepper to taste

Place rinsed and drained roast beef in medium sized bowl. Add salsa fresca, salt and pepper. Shred the beef while mixing in the other ingredients until it has a stringy texture. Heat in small saucepan on medium low heat until hot. This makes about 1 1/2 cups shredded beef, or enough for eight tacos or tostadas, or four burritos.

THE PURIST'S TRADITIONAL SHREDDED BEEF:

1 4 - 5 pound pot roast
1/4 cup flour
2 tbsp corn or canola oil
1 large onion, chopped
1 cup water
3 cloves garlic, minced
1 can pureed tomatoes
1 cup salsa fresca
1 tbsp beef bouillon
1 tsp each cayenne pepper, chili powder and oregano

Dredge pot roast in flour. In a Dutch oven, heat oil until sizzling. Brown pot roast on all sides in oil. Remove roast from pot, add onions and cook until translucent. Put roast back in pot. Add water, garlic and all other ingredients. Stir well. Bring to boil. Cover and reduce heat. Simmer for at least four hours, until meat is fork tender. Remove from heat and cool until you are able to comfortably handle meat. Place meat on cutting board and using two forks, shred the beef. Return meat to pan and stir with all spices.

You have enough shredded beef for two dozen tacos or tostadas, or about fifteen to eighteen burritos. Any unused meat can be frozen for future use.

CHICKEN FILLING for TACOS, BURRITOS & TOSTADAS

Use this filling in any of the taco, tostada or burrito recipes. It's a lean, lighter way to fill your tortillas, but I guarantee you, you won't be sacrificing any flavor! You'll have enough chicken filling to make 12 tacos or tostadas, or about eight burritos.

2 pounds boneless skinless chicken breasts -or-
2 12 ounce cans white meat chicken
1/2 to 1 cup salsa fresca
2 cloves garlic, minced
salt and pepper to taste

Bake chicken breasts in oven for 30 minutes at 350 degrees. Remove from oven and cool. Using two forks, shred the chicken. If you are using canned chicken, drain off excess liquid, place in bowl and shred.

In a medium sized bowl, mix shredded chicken with salsa and garlic. Add salt and pepper to taste.

TURKEY FILLING for TACOS, BURRITOS & TOSTADAS

Use this filling in any of the taco, tostada or burrito recipes. It's lean and light, yet delicious. Thanks to the cumin you'll never taste anything that compares to this turkey filling. It's delectable! You'll have enough filling to make 12 tacos or tostadas, or about eight burritos.

2 pounds white turkey meat
1/2 cup salsa fresca
2 cloves garlic, minced
2 tsp ground cumin
Pico Pica sauce or any red pepper sauce to taste
salt and pepper to taste

Bake turkey in oven for 30 minutes at 350 degrees. Remove from oven and cool. Using two forks, shred the turkey. In a medium sized bowl, mix shredded turkey with salsa, garlic, cumin, Pico Pica sauce, salt and pepper. Serve.

FISH TACOS

This Baja creation has been around longer than I have. According to local legend, fish tacos originated in San Felipe where they have always been the street taco of choice. In the early 80's, they were discovered by a young Baja aficionado who pirated the recipe from a now defunct taco vendor and bought it northwest to San Diego. He opened a tiny taco shop named Rubio's down by Mission Bay that specialized in authentic Baja-style fish tacos. By the year 2000 it's expected that there will be over 100 Rubio's restaurants in Southern California — so I guess I don't really need to tell you that the popularity of those fish tacos has skyrocketed.

For the best fish tacos south of the border these days, (in Nina's opinion) you have to travel to San Felipe (on the Sea of Cortez) or Ensenada (directly west on the Pacific). Her favorite tacos can be found at the fish market in Ensenada. When you first drive into town, you'll make a right turn just past the ship repair yards and immediately you'll see the outdoor fish market. There's a huge palapa on the right, at dockside, where vendors sell an incredible array of just-caught seafood, fresh shrimp cocktails and the most awesome fish tacos around. In case you're wondering, Juan Carlos, the grinning gato, agrees with Nina 100%. He does so love those fish tacos, he comes all the way up from his new home in Todos Santos to Ensenada at least twice a year just to eat some!

 This recipe does its best to bring Baja Fish Tacos to you without using a deep fryer and heavy batter. Depending on their appetites, this will serve three to four people. But then again — if your friends are anything like ours — they may be so enamored with your fish tacos that you'll have to double the recipe next time around. You could have worse problems! Oh, and if you don't want to use fried fish, you can lightly season and broil or grill the fish filets instead. You won't sacrifice either the taste or the inherent air of festivity generated by these colorful, incredible tacos.

8 filets of white fish, cut into strips of about 1 1/2" x 4" each
1/2 cup corn flake crumbs
1/4 cup Italian bread crumbs
2 eggs, lightly beaten
1/2 cup corn or canola oil
1 cup thin sour cream sauce

sauce to taste
6 radishes, minced
1 cup shredded cabbage for garnish (use a mixture of purple and green)
1/2 bunch cilantro, in sprigs
1 large tomato, chopped
1 cup Cheddar, Chihuahua or Jack cheese, shredded
salsa fresca to taste

Dredge each fish filet in beaten egg. Coat thoroughly with mixture of corn flake crumbs and Italian bread crumbs. In a frying pan heat oil until a drop of water sizzles when put in the pan.

Cook each fish filet for three to four minutes on each side. Remove from pan and drain on paper towels. Place filets in oven on warm until you are ready to serve.

In a small bowl, mix the sour cream sauce and Pico Pica with the radishes. Put a fish filet on one half of a hot corn tortilla. Place one to two tablespoons of sauce on top of filet as you are serving it. Garnish with shredded cabbage and serve immediately with salsa fresca on the side.

BAY OF L.A. LOBSTER TACOS

The first time I ever heard of lobster tacos was at Mama Diaz' restaurant in Bahía de Los Angeles. (Bay of L.A., as we gringos call it, is a remote but spectacularly scenic fishing village on the Sea of Cortez, a third of the way down the Baja peninsula.) That trip was almost thirty years ago, before there was even a paved road south of El Rosario (barely the other side of Ensenada).

We flew in with Francisco (Pancho) Muñoz, a World War II ace who ran Baja Airlines and was a great buddy of both my Pappy and Erle Stanley Gardner. Pancho's leaflets advertised the Bay of L.A. as, " ... the Fabulous Fishing Resort in Baja." A flight left Tijuana every Friday morning at 11:00 and returned every Saturday at 2:00 pm. Round trip tickets went for $47.52. Flying time was a little over two hours in one of his two Douglas B-18's (World War II cargo planes similar to DC-3's). After we'd traveled with Muñoz a few times, he and my dad (who were the same age) became great amigos in their own right. Often, over the years,

when we flew with him, one of my folks would sit up in the cockpit and hang out with him. Sometimes Nina and I got to also, but our favorite jobs were when we got to serve canned drinks, sack lunches and other snacks to the passengers — which to two girls under 12 was — in today's gringo lingo — way cool.

I still think of Muñoz whenever I pass the airport in Ensenada and see a pair of old, dilapidated Douglas B-18's sitting beside the runway there, just rusting away. Every single time I wonder if those are his planes, the same planes I flew all over Baja in when I was a kid. I don't know. Muñoz has long since retired and is in his 70's now, but Nina and I will never forget him or his dare-devil landings, some of which were on dirt runways barely wider than a truck.

A few years ago I went back to the Bay of L.A. Sure enough, the Casa Diaz was still there, even though Mama and Antero had both passed away. And sure enough, they still served lobster tacos, even though they weren't on the menu. Some things don't ever change and one of those facts of life is that the best things in Mexico are not always on the menu! Especially in the obscure places. I like that. Lobster tacos are best served as soft tacos in fresh corn tortillas. Makes 12 tacos.

2 pounds cooked, diced lobster meat
2 cloves garlic, minced
2 serrano or jalapeño chiles, minced (hot)
1 tbsp fresh Mexican lime juice

Heat all ingredients in medium sized saucepan. Serve as you would any tacos with a variety of condiments.

LOS ARCOS CEVICHE TOSTADAS

At the very tip of Baja, just offshore from Cabo San Lucas, is what's called Finisterra, or Land's End. There is an exquisite beach that you can reach only by boat, whether it be panga, yacht, kayak or jet ski. It's a two-sided spit of sand called Lover's Beach and it gets pretty windy out there because one side of it faces the Pacific and the other the Sea of Cortez. Just past it is the world-famous, frequently-photographed, dramatic rock formations known as Los Arcos. These rocks rise ruggedly above an undersea cascade of rocks and sand which was discovered and explored by Jacques Cousteau a couple of decades back.

While Cabo San Lucas was visited by the missionaries as far back as the 1500's, and it was a favored hang out for pirates and whaling vessels in the 1800's, it really didn't take off as a town until the late 1960's. With the completion of Mexico's Highway 1, which runs down the entire length of the Baja peninsula in 1974, Cabo finally began to grow. The first time I vacationed there in the early 80's it was a sleepy village with absolutely zero night life. These days it's a bustling tourist metropolis that's home to both Planet Hollywood and the Hard Rock Cafe. Any night of the week you can hear young (and even some not-so-young) American tourists boogying the night away, hooting and hollering in any of the many bars and night clubs all over town.

When you go to Cabo, try one of these delicate, spicy and healthful snacks at any of the beach-front restaurants on El Medano Beach, the main beach in town. You can wiggle your toes in the warm sand as the sun sets behind you and watch as the sky turns from golden to flaming crimson to a delicate almost-orange and then fades out into sultry opalescence. While the waves lap gently in front you, sip an iced libation and munch on ceviche tostadas just like these. This recipe makes 12 tostadas and will serve six to eight.

6 cups ceviche (see recipe in Appetizer section)
12 fried flat tortillas

Spoon the chilled ceviche directly onto fried flat tortillas. Top with all tostada toppings except frijoles. Serve immediately.

ENCHILADAS & RELLENOS

© Bob Bonn 1997

Tres Palmas

Enchiladas and Chiles Rellenos are two more typical Mexican dishes I grew up eating — and loving. While I remember having a choice between beef, chicken or cheese enchiladas at local Mexican restaurants when I was younger, there was only one kind of chile relleno around back then. It was a green chile stuffed with white cheese, fried in egg batter and smothered with a mild salsa.

That original relleno is still my favorite. But I have discovered that my basic Mexican chile relleno has some pretty exotic relatives. They've come out of the woodwork in recent years to grace the menus of gourmet restaurants in Baja and mainland Mexico as well as the fancy Southwestern eateries north of the border.

As these entrees have been continuously and mystically altered by creative chefs, I've struggled to keep up. I have managed to come up with a few elegant variations of enchiladas and rellenos. But — to tell you the truth — I've only succeeded as much as I want to succeed at this. **Cooking With Baja Magic** isn't supposed to be a gourmet cookbook, full of recipes that take all day to make. Not even!

So, please be assured that I don't want you to be frustrated. I don't want you to plan a fiesta and be utterly exhausted by the time the guests arrive. Or worse yet, I don't want you to cancel the entire party at the last minute (or throw everything in the trash and order pizzas) because dinner didn't turn out. That isn't what Baja Magic is about! Baja Magic is about having fun. It's about going barefoot, putting a flower behind your ear and dancing around the kitchen to La Bamba de Vera Cruz as you dip your tortillas into a wonderful, smooth, toma-toey-smelling sauce and fill those soon-to-be-enchiladas with chicken, olives and onions.

Anyway — I've offered you a combination of the old standbys and a few of the newer, snazzier versions of enchiladas and rellenos. Plus you get to take another trip with me down Memory Lane to the El Dorado Restaurant on the sand in Puerto Vallarta, where one of my mom's and my all-time favorite dishes was born. Chilequiles. Do try that one! And, please — don't worry. As always, my recipes are simple to prepare without sacrificing flavor and excitement.

Just remember — take off your shoes before you start to cook. Barefoot is necessary. It loosens you up and lets the slightly offbeat, eccentric, playful imp inside you come out to play. And that is critical if you are to evolve into a real Baja chef!

© Bob Bonn 1997

CHICKEN ENCHILADAS SUIZAS

I first had these mild, yet flavorful enchiladas when I was ten years old and staying in La Paz for the very first time. Enchiladas are the top of the line as far as Mexican food goes, according to my mom (and her mom before her). So of course I was encouraged to try them on my first big Baja adventure. I loved them then and I love them now. In fact, the most recent time I had Enchiladas Suizas was at a bay-front restaurant right on the malecón in Lap Paz — for breakfast!

I couldn't believe they were really and truly on the breakfast menu, but they were. And I, preferring enchiladas to eggs most any day, promptly ordered them. Of course, this story wouldn't be complete if I didn't tell you what Nina ordered. She ordered a "Perrito Caliente," which was a huge hot dog, (although the literal translation is "warm puppy") smothered in mustard and loaded up with cheese, bacon, pineapple and avocado. For breakfast, mind you. For breakfast! With coffee!

While I haven't included this recipe in the breakfast section (and I certainly didn't add the warm puppy to this book!) I do recommend these enchiladas for breakfast, lunch or dinner. This recipe serves four.

1 20 ounce can whole tomatoes
1 7 ounce can diced green chiles
1 medium onion, quartered
2 - 3 cloves garlic, peeled
1 cup thick sour cream sauce (from Salsa section)
salt and pepper to taste
12 corn tortillas
1/2 cup corn or canola oil
2 pounds boneless chicken breasts, cooked and cubed
4 cups Swiss, Chihuahua or Jack cheese, grated
1 bunch green onions, chopped
1 cup thin sour cream sauce (from Salsa section)

In food processor, blend together tomatoes, chiles, onion, garlic and sour cream sauce. Season to taste with salt and pepper and pour into a large saucepan. Heat thoroughly.

Heat oil in skillet until a drop of water sizzles when placed in it. Fry a tortilla lightly on both sides so it's still pliable. Using tongs, remove it from the pan. Dip it into the enchilada sauce and lay it inside a 9 x 14 pan. Stuff enchilada with chicken, cheese and onions. Roll and place seam side down in the pan. Repeat for all 12 tortillas, reserving a small amount of cheese and onions.

When all enchiladas are made, place the pan in a 350 degree oven for about twenty minutes. Remove from oven, pour remaining enchilada sauce over enchiladas until almost covered. Cover with remaining cheese and onions. Broil for two minutes or until cheese is melted. Serve immediately, topped with thin sour cream sauce.

CHICKEN ENCHILADAS VERDES

After my son Derek was born, a friend of mine brought this dish over to us for dinner one night. I loved it and immediately called to ask her where she'd gotten the recipe. Amazingly enough, she'd had these enchiladas with a tangy green sauce at a fancy restaurant in Ensenada while on one of those three-day cruises to Baja. She, like my mother and me before her, had begged the recipe off her waiter and brought it home with her to add to her repertory. Since she shared it

with me, I can now share it with you and you too can enjoy these enchiladas with a true Baja flair. Serves six.

Sour Cream-Chile Sauce:
1 pint sour cream
1 can cream of chicken soup
1 1/2 cups salsa verde
1 7 ounce can diced green chiles

Enchiladas:
2 bunches green onions, chopped
4 cups Chihuahua or Jack cheese, shredded
18 corn tortillas
2 pounds boneless chicken breasts, cooked and cubed.
1 additional cup of salsa verde

To make sauce, combine sour cream, chicken soup, salsa verde and green chiles in a medium sized bowl and stir well. Set aside.

Heat oil in skillet until a drop of water sizzles when placed in the pan. Fry a tortilla lightly on both sides so it is still pliable. Using tongs, remove it from the pan and drain on paper towels. Lay it inside a 9 x 14 pan. Place a tablespoon of sauce on each dipped tortilla. Top with chicken, cheese and onions. Roll and place seam down in pan.

When all tortillas are filled, mix left over sauce with additional cup of salsa verde. Pour over enchiladas. Top with remaining cheese and onions. Bake at 300 degrees for twenty minutes or until cheese is melted.

CHILEQUILES VALLARTA

We used to eat Chilequiles at the El Dorado Restaurant in Puerto Vallarta when I was a kid. We sat in yellow and green chairs right on the sand and ate at low tables in our wet bathing suits. To this day, whenever I go to Puerto Vallarta, the El Dorado is one of my first stops. Even though the resort has grown astronomically and bears little resemblance to the sleepy village Nina, our parents and I remember from the 60's, the El Dorado is still there and it still serves some of the best food in Puerto Vallarta. And hey, there's no way you can beat the location!

One of my favorite memories from the El Dorado dates back to the Christmas of 1967. We had just ordered lunch. My parents were discussing the concept of the empty nest. I could tell that my dad was wor- ried about my mom being lonely as he anticipated Nina's and my eventual departure for college. Suddenly he stood up. My eyes followed his until I spotted the cutest little black and white puppy I had ever set eyes on. It was under the pier, on a frayed rope held by one of two little Mexican girls. Within two minutes my dad had bought that dog for $4.00 U.S., plus a few pesos to buy ice cream for the crying little girls. We named her Victoria, and she was my mother's shadow for the next 16 years.

Meanwhile, back on the beach, Victoria fell asleep in Nina's lap. Our lunch arrived and we dug in. Nina's attention got diverted by a beach vendor selling silver earrings, necklaces and rings. When she looked back down at her plate, her chilequiles were gone. Little Victoria, barely six weeks old, had scarfed the entire meal!

Chilequiles were, and still are, a favorite of mine. They're served all over Baja and are offered on most break- fast menus as a local alternative to eggs and such. I maintain that like Enchiladas Suizas, you can eat them for breakfast, lunch or dinner. They are that versatile! Oh, and by the way — Victoria flew home with us on Muñoz' Baja Airlines. Unlike a pet on an

American airliner, she wasn't treated like a piece of luggage and relegated to the baggage department. Nope. Not her. Instead, she napped on the seat next to me and chased my dad up and down the aisle, barking gleefully as he helped hand out sack lunches. This recipe serves six and it will make you think you're right there on the sand, within steps of that 80 degree ocean. Oh yeah!

1 1/2 pounds boneless chicken breasts, cooked and cut in chunks
12 corn tortillas
1/2 cup corn oil
1 7 ounce can green chiles, cut in strips
4 cups Chihuahua or Jack cheese, grated
2 cups enchilada sauce (use my recipe from Enchiladas Suizas, Taos Enchilada Sauce or canned sauce)
1 cup sour cream
1/2 cup thin sour cream sauce

Cut tortillas into one inch strips and fry in oil until crisp. Drain on paper towels. Combine enchilada sauce with sour cream in saucepan. Heat thoroughly.

In a 9 x 11 pan layer the tortilla strips, chicken, chile strips, cheese and enchilada sauce. Repeat. Top with a layer of tortilla strips, sauce and lots of cheese. Bake at 350 degrees for 25 minutes or until cheese is melted and chilequiles are bubbling. Pour thin sour cream sauce over each serving.

CHILES RELLENOS

Sue and Jim are about my age. They're former urban professionals who have ducked out of the rat race and expatriated themselves to Baja. There they act as co-presidents of the La Bufadora Adventurers Club — a very loosely knit group of us who love to kayak, snorkel, hike or just hang around on the beach. We have a lot of fun together. In fact, my kids and I always look forward to honking our horn at them whenever we glide into town on Friday afternoons at sunset, so we can plan some major adventures for the weekend. Sometimes, however, when we come down, they're gone. Where'd they go? you ask. Why — gallivanting around Baja — of course — the rascals. (Can you tell how envious I am?! I am. I am. I am.)

This is Sue's incredible chiles rellenos recipe. She insisted I use it because it's far better than the one I invented back in college. I had a phobia about blistering and skinning chiles, so I used canned chiles instead of fresh in my recipe. "Naughty, naughty," said Sue, shaking her head in disbelief. She proceeded to teach me how to blister and skin those chiles, and now I will teach you! Serves six.

6 large pasilla (also called ancho) chiles (spicy) -or-
6 large Anaheim chiles (much milder)
1/2 pound Chihuahua or Jack cheese, thinly sliced
1/4 cup flour
6 raw eggs, separated
1/2 cup flour
1/4 tsp salt
2 cups salsa verde (Sue uses Herdez Salsa Verde) -or-
2 cups Pancho's Salsa Ranchera (Mary's way see recipe in the salsa section)
1 cup corn or canola oil

To blister chiles, cook over a gas burner, turning constantly until they're evenly charred and stop making popping sounds. Wrap each chile in a paper towel and moisten with water to steam. After a few minutes, peel skin off chile and cut a slit almost the full length of each chile. Make a small "t" across the top, by the stem. Pull out fibers and seeds (the seeds are where the heat is) and replace with a slice of cheese.

Whip egg whites at high speed until stiff peaks have formed. (Sue does this by hand with a wire whisk.) At the same time, heat the oil in a skillet until a drop of water sizzles when put into pan. Beat egg yolks with one tablespoon flour and salt. mix into egg whites and stir until you have a thick paste.

Roll chiles in 1/4 cup flour and dip in egg batter, seam side down. Fry on both sides, then drain on paper towels. Meanwhile, heat salsa (either one or some of each) and pour over chiles rellenos. Serve immediately with carne asada, enchiladas or carnitas as a split entree. Or serve alone and savor the flavor. I can't even begin to tell you how good these are!

STACKED CHEESE ENCHILADAS TAOS STYLE

New Mexico chiles and cinnamon give these stacked enchiladas a flavor that is singularly Southwestern. I first tasted enchiladas prepared this way on a trip to Taos, New Mexico in 1980. I never ran into Juan Carlos on that trip — I don't think he was born yet. But I do still clearly remember that chilly winter evening as my boyfriend and I dined in a 400 year-old adobe building in the Old Taos Pueblo. We could have been in a museum, there were so many Native American artifacts around us. Navajo rugs, Hopi and Zuni kachina dolls and Pueblo pottery and baskets. A kiva, or round stucco fireplace dominated the room. From it radiated a wonderful, cozy warmth.

My stomach growled as my nose caught wind of the aromas drifting in from behind the swinging kitchen doors. There was one smell in particular that intrigued me and I asked our waiter what it was. (Can you guess?!) These unusual enchiladas are still as good as they smelled that night. Even though there's nothing Baja about them, they are so incredible that I couldn't resist sneaking them into this book! They make an attractive and not-often-seen presentation, especially if you use blue corn tortillas. Overall, they're easier to make than rolled enchiladas and the fried egg on top makes for a diner's delight. Serves four.

Taos Style Enchilada Sauce:
12 - 20 seeded dried red New Mexico chiles (hot) -or- 4 - 6 tbsp New Mexico chiles

Mexico chili powder(hot) or 4-6 tbsp American chile powder (this is much milder)
3 cloves garlic, minced
1 medium onion, quartered
1 tsp cinnamon
1 tbsp sugar
2 12 ounce cans tomato sauce
salt and pepper to taste

Stacked Enchiladas:
12 blue corn or regular corn tortillas
1 cup corn or canola oil
1 large onion, chopped
4 cups cheddar cheese, shredded
3 tbsp butter
4 eggs
4 green onions, diced
1 3 1/2 ounce can sliced black olives
1 cup shredded lettuce
1 fresh avocado, diced

Remove stems and seeds from chiles. In a medium sauce pan, simmer chiles in 3/4 cup water for ten minutes or until tender. Puree in food processor with garlic, onion, cinnamon and sugar. (If you're using powdered chiles, puree all ingredients including tomato sauce and an additional 1/2 cup water in food processor.) Return to sauce pan. Add tomato sauce, salt and pepper. Simmer for 20 minutes to an hour.

Heat oil in small skillet. Fry each tortilla until slightly crisp. Dip each tortilla in enough enchilada sauce to lightly coat it. After you dip the first four tortillas, place them side by side in a large, greased pan. Sprinkle with a tablespoon of onion and 1/4 cup cheese. Fry the next tortilla, dip in sauce and lay over the first tortilla and filling. Sprinkle on more onion and cheese. Fry, dip and lay on the third and last tortilla of each stack. Sprinkle the remaining cheese on top of each stack.

Fry the eggs three minutes in butter. Lift each stack, using a wide spatula to waiting dinner plates. Top with fried egg and garnish with minced green onion, olives shredded lettuce and diced avocado.

CRAB ENCHILADAS CALAFIA STYLE

A few minutes south of Rosarito on the free road (no tolls) is the resort, Calafia. It has been around for as long as I can remember and is famous for its rocking and rolling pirate ship, painted in an array of wild colors that hangs precariously out over a hot surf spot on the Pacific Ocean. The deejay actually plays his music from inside

the ship as revelers dance the afternoons and nights away on its wooden decks or on one of the restaurant's many patios.

More sedate or hungry people can order lunch at one of the many outdoor tables terraced down the side of the cliff, overlooking the crashing waves (and the dancers). This recipe for Crab Enchiladas was inspired by one of our escapades to Calafia. They've become a big time favorite in Northern Baja as well as in Southern California, where seafood and Mexican food enjoy a symbiotic relationship, and Nina was dying to get the recipe. So she ordered them, but she was the only one who did. When our food arrived, Nina raved about these enchiladas with such enthusiasm that the other people in our group began attacking her plate and nearly wiped it out before she could finish a single enchilada! In our family we've always called that the "wandering fork game" and Nina has always been our star player, as her fork can dart in and out of other people's meals faster than anyone I've ever known. This time it was kind of amusing to see the tables turned on her.

Because the waiter refused to give us the recipe, we proceeded to analyze the ingredients. After a bit of trial and error in the kitchen, this recipe was born. These Crab Enchiladas are delicate, unique and — as Nina will absolutely guarantee you — if you serve them with frijoles negros and wilted cabbage salad, you'll have a real hit on your hands. Serves four.

1 tbsp butter or margarine
1 tbsp corn or canola oil
2 garlic cloves and 1 medium onion, minced
1 tbsp American chili powder
1 1/2 pounds fresh cooked crab meat
1/3 cup mayonnaise (non-fat is okay)
1/2 tsp salt
1 tbsp cilantro, chopped
12 corn tortillas
3 cups enchilada sauce (use either of mine, or canned)
1/2 cup corn or canola oil (to fry tortillas)
4 cups Chihuahua or Jack cheese, grated
1 bunch green onions, chopped

Melt butter and oil in a medium saucepan over low heat. Add garlic and onion and cook over medium heat until translucent. Remove from heat and add chili powder, crab, mayonnaise, salt and cilantro. Heat enchilada sauce in another saucepan.

In a skillet, heat oil until a drop of water sizzles when placed in the pan. Fry a tortilla lightly on both sides so it is still pliable. Using tongs, remove it from the pan. Dip it into the enchilada sauce and lay it inside a 9 x 14 pan. Stuff enchilada with crab mixture, cheese and onions. Roll and place seam side down in the pan. Repeat with all tortillas. When all enchiladas are made, place the pan in a 350 degree oven for about twenty minutes. Remove from oven, pour remaining enchilada sauce over enchiladas until almost covered. Top with remaining cheese and onions. Broil for one to two minutes until cheese is melted. Serve immediately and await compliments.

CARNITAS ENCHILADAS

This simple enchiladas dish is festive, new on the Baja scene and fabulous. It's a perfect way to use up left over carnitas, which if you recall, I am quite partial to. So you can bet that I invariably find myself in a good mood whenever I'm getting ready to make Carnitas Enchiladas. I especially like the salsa verde instead of enchilada sauce in this dish, because its tart but zesty flavor complements the pork perfectly.

Serve guacamole and chips before-hand with these enchiladas and try a chilled Gazpacho Rojo instead of salad. Round everything out with White Rice with Vegetables and you will have yourself a Baja style feast. I'm salivating already — are you?! Serves four.

1 1/2 pounds left over carnitas
12 corn tortillas
1/2 cup corn or canola oil
2 cups Chihuahua or Jack cheese, grated
2 - 3 cups salsa verde
1 cup thin sour cream sauce
paprika as garnish

Heat carnitas meat in saucepan until hot. Preheat oven to 400 degrees. Heat oil in heavy skillet until a drop of water sizzles when placed in it. Using tongs, cook a tortilla until pliable. Drain on paper towels. Place two tablespoons carnitas meat and some cheese inside the tortilla. Roll and place, seam side down in baking dish. Repeat.

Sprinkle remaining cheese over the enchiladas and place in oven until cheese is melted. Pour salsa verde and thin sour cream sauce over the enchiladas. Garnish with paprika. Serve immediately.

BAJA

MAGIC

SEAFOOD ENTREES

Cat Fishing

California and Baja California coexist on over 3,000 miles of coastline — not counting any of the zigs and zags. Off the west coast of both are the cool waters (55° - 70° Fahrenheit) of the Pacific. This ocean offers up lobster, abalone, tuna and halibut — to name only a few varieties of its bounty. The much warmer (usually 75° - 85° Fahrenheit) Sea of Cortez is a 1000 mile ocean trench that extends between Baja on the west and the Sierra de la Madre Mountains of mainland Mexico on the east. It's home to at least 850 known species of marine creatures, (the richest abundance of undersea life anywhere on the planet) ranging from shrimp to dorado to huachinango to tiburón to the magnificent marlin and sailfish.

Some of the best big game fishing in the world is found just north of Cabo San Lucas off the east coast of southernmost Baja. I know — my dad began taking us there when I was eight. Back in the early 60's when we first visited La Paz and the East Cape area just to the south of it, the only way to get in was by boat or by air. The paved road wasn't completed for another decade. Our friend Francisco Muñoz' Baja Airlines flew in from Tijuana, along with Aeronaves de Mexico and Mexicana de Aviación. No gringo airlines did. Muñoz carried his share of rich and famous Baja Aficionados down there to fish. Guys like Chuck Connors, Desi Arnaz, Fred Astaire and my Pappy's pal, Erle Stanley Gardner. Back then the waters churned with rooster fish, the wildest fighters in all of the Sea of Cortez — said to be even more exciting to reel in than a marlin.

I caught one. Nina caught one. My mom caught several. In fact, my mother likes to say that she, Nina and I were all over-fished before I was ten. An exaggeration? Probably not. I remember the Easter vacation when I was nine. We flew into La Paz on a Saturday. Before dawn on Sunday morning we were aboard a cabin cruiser, speeding towards fertile fishing grounds. My parents were on deck fishing until lunch. Nina and I got bored by 9:30 and by 11:30 we'd tasted our way through every cold burrito and cookie and sandwich in every single sack lunch on the boat! You can imagine our parents' embarrassment when they discovered we'd sampled pieces (a la Goldilocks) of everyone's food. My dad did his best to explain the situation in his fishing boat Spanish to our captain (who of course spoke no English). Finally, with my mom's help, he got the point across. The growling stomachs on board won out over any pretense of convention and everyone agreed that eating pre-tasted food was better than eating no food at all! So they ate. We, obviously, weren't hungry! By the time they'd finished lunch, it had all become a great joke. And one we laugh about to this day.

We were, by then, anchored off Isla Espiritú Santa, that huge multi-bayed island populated only by sea birds, sand, cacti, driftwood and shells — and surrounded by see-through aquamarine water. As I peered overboard, I glimpsed bright colors flashing against the current, as school after school of tropical fish darted below us. Mom taught us how to snorkel that day. Our next time out we found another deserted cove on the same island and picnicked there. We returned to the boat with our t-shirts fashioned into sacks that overflowed with sea shells. We fished four out of the five days we were there. To top off a great trip, we ran into John Wayne at the La Paz airport and Nina had her picture taken with him. We've been hooked on Baja ever since. When my dad had completely over-fished us, about five years later, he began making his annual fishing trips without us. He began going to Buena Vista on the East Cape with his brother, Bruce and a gang of their construction buddies instead.

These days we usually do a trip to Southern Baja once or twice a year. We usually fly into Los Cabos Airport because nine or ten major airlines fly into Los Cabos. The last time we landed there the tarmac was jam-packed! I counted nine planes lined up, in various stages of planing and deplaning. Things have changed — all the way around. There's more to do than just fish now. Nina and John prefer to go diving. Gayle and I prefer snorkeling and kayaking. Or climbing the only "mountain" around (make that a high hill) to catch the sunrise over the Sea of Cortez. My mom paints and reads. Only Derek has inherited his grandpa's passion for fishing. And every morning, they're up before dawn, slapping on the sunscreen, lugging their fishing poles down to the beach. Ready to fish!

This section offers up an abundance of seafood dishes. Some are spicy, some aren't. All come to you courtesy of Nina, the family seafood aficionada. They're all great. And guaranteed to transport you — south.

GARLIC SHRIMP ON SKEWERS

Garlic shrimp is my kids' dad's absolute favorite Baja dish. When we were married and traveled to Los Cabos, he'd eat it at least once a day. By the fourth day we had to turn the air conditioning off in our hotel room and leave all the windows open because I couldn't breathe when we were together in a closed room! He didn't even need to open his mouth! The garlic was so overpowering it literally oozed out his pores and swirled around in circles around him, like a really fragrant aura! (And no — that's not why we got divorced!)

This shrimp is skewered, saturated with garlic and cooked over hot coals. Serve with Ensalada Chileno Bay, Cantaloupe Soup and pitcher of fruity Margaritas for a scrumptious, tropical dinner. (But don't eat it twice a day for four days. Or you too will be too fragrant for your own good!) Serves six to eight.

3 pounds jumbo shrimp, deveined
2 - 4 tbsp minced garlic (depending on how brave you are)
1/4 cup white wine
1/4 cup lemon juice
1/2 bunch cilantro, stems removed and finely chopped
1/2 cup butter or margarine, melted
wooden skewers

In small bowl, combine garlic, wine, lemon juice, cilantro and melted butter or margarine. Place shrimp in 9 x 14 pan. Cover with marinade. Refrigerate one hour. When ready to barbecue, place the shrimp on skewers, making sure that they are well saturated with the marinade. Grill for three minutes on each side, basting frequently with marinade until done.

TÍO PABLO'S CABRILLA VERACRUZANA

Seaport resorts in Baja and mainland Mexico always offer fresh cabrilla (sea bass) or red snapper (huachinango) served this way. It's a timeless classic, full of nutritious vegetables and subtly spicy. Nina swears that the best Veracruzana she has ever, ever had is at Tío Pablos's Bar & Grill in Los Barriles — next to Buena Vista on the East Cape of Baja California del Sur.

This restaurant offers up the finest in patio dining in an old-fashioned Spanish courtyard setting. It's also a great place to escape the mid-day sun and grab a quick beer and fish taco under their palapa or in their Escorpión Bar. Go in on a weekday afternoon and you'll be amazed by all the resident gringas hanging out in the shade, sipping iced tea and munching on nachos (they're humongous and ever-so-good!) while playing Mah Jong. Really! The ambiance is pure Baja and the food is delicious. This meal serves four and at Tío's they serve it on a bed of fluffy rice.

4 tomatoes, sliced in half-moons
4 white onions, sliced in half-rings
1 8 ounce can pitted green olives
2 8 ounce cans tomato puree
3 green bell peppers, cut into strips
1 tsp oregano
1 tbsp salt, or to taste
1 tsp black pepper, or to taste
1/4 cup olive oil
2 cups water
4 tbsp butter or margarine
8 filets cabrilla, huachinango (or other delicate, firm white fish)
8 cloves garlic, minced

To make the Salsa Veracruzana:
Heat the oil, add the garlic and onions. Cook until onions are translucent. Add bell peppers and tomatoes, tomato puree, olive oil and seasonings and cook for five to eight minutes, or until the flavors are well-blended. Add the water to prevent sticking. Add olives the last three minutes.

In a large saute pan, melt the butter or margarine with the minced garlic. Saute fish until white and flaky. Smother the filets in the Salsa Veracruzana. Serve immediately, dig in and enjoy!

EAST CAPE SWORD-FISH IN CILANTRO BUTTER

Picture yourself dining on a balmy evening in February when the weather is worse than miserable stateside — on a terrace overlooking the sea in one of the chic multi-starred hotels that have popped up along the Sea of Cortez between San Jose del Cabo and Cabo San Lucas (known to the gringo population by the airport's name of Los Cabos).

No?! Oh. I get it. Your renegade spirit is

acting up, isn't it? You say you don't feel like dressing up for dinner? You want simple, not swanky? Okay. Then go back to the airport, get in a taxi and transport yourself about an hour north, to the gulf's fishing mecca — the East Cape. There, in casual-but-gorgeous, old-style hotels like the Buena Vista Beach Resort or the remote but breathtaking dive resort just down the beach, Rancho Leonero. From there you can catch a glimpse of the Baja California del Sur that used to be.

The pace is slower on the East Cape. It doesn't appeal to the crowd that flocks to Cabo to sip Piña Coladas at the swim-up bars by day, dine al fresco at night and dance until the wee hours at one of the plentiful night clubs and discos. (Although Cabo is great if that's what you're in the mood for.) It draws instead the fisher people and tranquility seekers — those of us who want to escape the rat race and get in touch with Mother Nature. Like I said, you don't have to dress for dinner. And, women — one of the best-kept secrets of non-resort Baja living is that after you do it for awhile, it's real likely that you'll forget panty hose ever existed. If you stay long enough, you won't even remember how to put on makeup. The thought of this may freak

freak you out at this moment in time, but I promise you — if you spend enough time in Baja (especially in off-the-beaten-track places) you will forget about things like mascara, blush — even lipstick ....

This delicate fish is wonderful served with Jicama Fresca, a Chopped Mexican Medley Salad or Molded Gazpacho, rolls and a glass of ice cold Chardonnay. (Or beer, if you're really feeling casual!) Serves six to eight and it is sure to please you, whether you're into high heels or going barefoot.

2 pounds swordfish (or 6 marlin or shark steaks)
1/4 cup white wine
2 tbsp Mexican lime juice
1 shot tequila
2 tbsp White Worcestershire Sauce for fish or chicken
1/4 cup salsa verde
1 tbsp minced garlic
1/2 cup butter or margarine
1/2 bunch cilantro, stems removed and finely chopped
salt and pepper to taste

In a 9 x 14 pan, pour wine, lime juice, tequila, Worcestershire Sauce and salsa verde over swordfish steaks. Marinate in refrigerator from one to two hours. Remove swordfish from

marinade and grill on barbecue for four minutes on each side, or until done.

While swordfish is grilling, melt butter or margarine in a small saucepan with garlic powder, cilantro, salt and pepper. Immediately prior to serving, pour equal amounts of butter sauce over each piece of fish. Serve immediately.

ISLA ESPIRTÚ SANTA PRAWNS WITH SALSA

Directly to the west of La Paz is a large island with at least 12 separate, pristine, uninhabited bays. When I saw them from the airplane on a recent flight south, I counted. Twelve — and I only counted the big ones. On the west side. This island, named after the Holy Spirit, is famous with divers all over the world. You can catch a dive ship from downtown La Paz, or at any of the local hotels. You can pick your bay. Or you can dive or snorkel with the sea lions that live at the north end of the island.

Whether you're a diver, a snorkeler, an avid fisher person or just a Baja cruiser, Espirtú Santa Island is a must-see. We visited many of its bays on our forays out into La Paz Bay when I was young. They still offer up the amazing undersea life and equally amazing shell-hunting on land that they did 35 years ago!

This spicy, saucy dish is pure La Paz. More cosmopolitan and sophisticated than the usual Baja fare, you will find it worthy of any five star resort. So, hey, dress up tonight and try this for a dinner party with an upscale Southern Baja flair. You'll love the unusual flavor of the shrimp. Served on a bed of rice, it's almost a full meal in itself. Precede it with a medley of appetizers and serve with a Marinated vegetable salad, Sinful Cinnamon Rice and Corona with a lime or a chilled Chenin Blanc. Elegant! Serves six.

2 pounds jumbo shrimp
1 1/2 cups white wine
1 cup water
2 tbsp minced garlic
1 tsp lemon juice
2 cups salsa fresca
8 cups hot cooked rice
cilantro sprigs for garnish
lemon or Mexican lime wedges for garnish

In large sauce pan, cover shrimp with wine and water. Bring mixture to a boil. Add garlic and lemon. Cook three

to five minutes until shrimp turn pink. Drain shrimp. Rinse well with cold water. Shell and devein shrimp.

Heat salsa in small saucepan. Serve shrimp on a bed of white rice topped with heated salsa. Garnish with cilantro and lemon slices.

LOBSTER PUERTO NUEVO

Thirty miles south of the Tijuana border is what used to be a fishing village called Puerto Nuevo (or Newport in English). In recent years its size has multiplied many times over until it has reached resort proportions. Puerto Nuevo is renowned throughout Southern California for its succulent lobster. In the old days, local fishermen cruised the shoreline in their pangas (two men motor skiffs) and free dove for the lobster off the rocks — often without wet suits — or scuba gear in the fall when the ocean wasn't exactly at its warmest.

These days everything's a little more sophisticated, but the lobster is still fresh and delicious. There are lots of big restaurants in Puerto Nuevo now,

most of which are named "Ortega's," but when I first went there in the late seventies, there were only three plywood and tar paper shacks with dirt floors that served lobster this way. And what they served the lobster with back then was nothing more than refried beans and corn tortillas. So guess what I had?!

Puerto Nuevo lobster is deep fried in lard, the Mexican way. If you don't want to fry your lobster, try grilling it on the barbecue or boiling it in water plus a half cup of beer for five minutes. When served with beans, rice, tortillas, Wilted Cabbage Salad and an array of different salsas, the meal takes on a festive atmosphere all its own. Frosty beers or Cokes a must with this one. Serves six to eight.

6 large Mexican lobsters, cut in half lengthwise
2 cups lard or solid vegetable shortening (optional: see above)
1 tbsp seasoned salt
1 tsp pepper
2 cups frijoles
2 cups Spanish rice
18 corn and/or flour tortillas
2 cups salsa fresca
1 cup salsa verde

In heavy, deep skillet heat lard over medium high heat. Fry each half lobster for five minutes on each side, until meat is crisp, tender and will pop out of the shell on your fork. Continue for all lobsters. Drain on paper towels and place on serving dish in the oven on warm until ready to serve.

Heat frijoles and rice. Place in serving dishes. Heat tortillas In microwave one to two minutes until warm. Place in covered bread basket. Serve lobster with frijoles, rice, tortillas, salsas. People can eat the lobster either in a burrito with beans and salsa, or solo.

The Mexicans use tortillas the way our ancestors used bread, to scoop up and mop up their beans, rice, excess pan juices and salsa. Try it out yourself.

CHIPOTLE SEA BASS WITH VEGETABLES

This is one of Nina's most sought-after dishes. She created it herself after a trip to Los Cabos one year, but she won't tell which restaurant she copied the recipe from. In fact, she swears she made it up all by herself!

Who am I to question the origins of this dish?! Even my son, the salsa phobic Derek raves about it. Because the sea bass (it's called cabrilla in Mexico) and vegetables are baked together with wine, chipotle chiles and cilantro, the fish takes on a distinctive, mouth-watering flavor. Zucchini with Corn and Peppers and a Watermelon Fruit Salad complete this meal. Serves six.

2 pounds sea bass, or 6 fillets
salt and pepper to taste
1 - 2 tbsp minced garlic
2 - 3 chipotle chiles, diced (available canned in adobo)
2 1/2 lemons, quartered
1/2 cup butter or margarine
1 onion, thinly sliced
2 medium potatoes, peeled and very thinly sliced
2 tomatoes, peeled and quartered
1/3 cup white wine
3 tbsp chopped cilantro

Season fish on both sides with salt and pepper, garlic and lemon juice. Sprinkle diced chipotle chiles over top. Melt butter in large skillet. Brown fish on both sides.

Transfer fish and juices to a 9 x 14 inch baking pan. Arrange onion and potato slices around fish and bake at 375 degrees for 30 minutes. Add tomatoes, pour wine over fish and sprinkle with cilantro. Bake ten minutes, or until fish flakes easily with fork and potatoes are done.

Arrange fish on large platter with tomatoes, potatoes and onions. Pour juices over fish and sprinkle with cilantro. Garnish with remaining lemon quarters.

BATTER FRIED SHRIMP MAZATLÁN STYLE

Mazatlán is a busy seaport and industrial city on the west coast of mainland Mexico just south of the tip of Baja. It was one of Mexico's first beach resorts back in the early 60's and is still a major stop on all Mexican Riviera cruises. We spent a few Easter vacations in Mazatlán when I was a kid, enjoying the sunny weather, warm water and friendly ambience.

The last time I was there, every night the tourists converged en masse on one of the town's premier eateries, the Shrimp Bucket. My father swears it has the best fried shrimp served anywhere. This is Nina's version of the dish, which she and my Mom and Dad made up together. Try it with Wilted Cabbage Salad and Papas Fritas con Chile Verde. Don't forget the cerveza! Serves six.

2 eggs, beaten
2 tbsp lemon juice
2 tbsp chopped cilantro
1 1/2 cups Italian bread crumbs
1 1/2 cups corn or canola oil
2 pounds jumbo shrimp, shelled and deveined

1 - 2 tbsp minced garlic
1 tbsp seasoned salt

In small bowl, mix eggs, lemon juice and cilantro. Dip each shrimp into the egg mixture and dredge in bread crumbs combined with garlic powder and seasoned salt.

Heat oil in skillet over medium high heat. Fry each shrimp about two to three minutes, or until crisp and golden. Drain on paper towels and place on platter in oven on warm until ready to serve.

SHARK STEAKS SANTA ROSALÍA

Santa Rosalía, almost two thirds of the way down the Baja coast is the only place in Baja with a French heritage. It was first occupied by the French in the 1870's and for nearly 80 years flourished as a manganese mining town. Its church is still world-famous. It was designed by Gustav Effeil for the Paris World's Fair in 1898 and actually constructed by one of his fellow students. After the fair's completion, the church was dismantled and shipped in pieces to Santa Rosalía around Cape Horn.

These days the town still has the best bakeries in all of Mexico, the most famous being El Boleo, named after the French Mining Company that settled it. It has a new marina and has begun to attract a few yachties that travel the Sea of Cortez in their sail and power boats during the pleasant fall, winter and late spring months. Other than that, Santa Rosalía is pretty much off the beaten tourist path as no major airlines fly in there. Caravans of motor homing travelers stop in to rest and stock up on supplies. A few folks, old school Baja Rats, the serious peace-and-quiet seekers, come to fish and hang out a while. Others stop in to catch the ferry to Guyamas on the mainland.

One of our yachtie friends brought this recipe back from a trip up the Sea of Cortez a few years back. Its simplicity is authenticlly Baja — with just a the hint of that French flair! Never eaten shark, you say? Well, most culinary experts, including — of course — our resident expert, Nina, swear it's as good as or better than swordfish. Even though it's served at all the best seafood restaurants in Baja and Southern California, our yachtie friend swears that she heard a rumor that it was a French miner, living in Santa Rosalía, who was the first one to have the courage to eat a shark. Whatever the truth may be, this quick and incredibly easy recipe for grilled shark steaks is a sure winner. It works just as well for an elegant dinner al fresco as it does for a shorts, t-shirts and bare feet affair. Choose your own array of accompaniments. Serves six.

2 pounds shark fillets or steaks
salt and pepper to taste
dash paprika and cayenne pepper
1/2 cup butter or margarine
2 tbsp lemon or Mexican lime juice
1 - 2 cloves garlic, minced
1 tbsp cilantro, chopped

Season fish fillets to taste with salt, pepper, paprika and cayenne. Melt butter in saucepan and add lemon or lime juice and garlic. Gently pour lemon butter over fish. Grill on barbecue on both sides until fish flakes easily when tested with a fork. Garnish with chopped cilantro.

SWORDFISH ISLA SAN JOSE

Just about midway between Loreto and La Paz on the Sea of Cortez is an island called Isla San Jose. Quiet and off the beaten track, it's a place visited mostly by fishermen, kayakers and other serious wildlife buffs (they call us eco-tourists these days!). My dad told me once that the biggest and widest variety of billfish once hung out in that area. Supposedly they were over-fished and pretty much disappeared from the area about 20 years ago — before tag and release programs became popular and did much to curb the wasteful slaughter of game fish in Baja.

Swordfish Isla San Jose is a tangy, baked dish that takes little time, but will get you rave reviews. You can substitute shark or tuna for the swordfish if you feel like it. And once again, you can pick and choose your side dishes. Get a little creative. Surprise yourself! Why not?! You could be in Baja, anchored off this exquisite, pristine island, with only the sea, stars and sky to observe you as you dance barefooted after dinner in the moonlight on the deck of your yacht. Hey?! Why not?! Can I come too?! Serves six.

6 swordfish steaks (can substitute 6 shark or tuna steaks)
salt and pepper to taste
6 tbsp olive oil
1 cup sliced green onions, tops included
1 1/2 limes, quartered
1 tomato, cut in six wedges
3 tbsp chopped cilantro

Sprinkle swordfish steaks with salt and pepper. Place fish in a single layer in 9 x 14 inch baking dish. Coat each steak heavily with olive oil. Sprinkle green onions over fish. Bake, uncovered at 350 degrees for about 20 minutes, or until fish flakes easily when tested with fork. Remove to serving platter. Sprinkle with cilantro and garnish with lime and tomato wedges.

ISLA CERALVO CINNAMON-CHILE SNAPPER

If you cruise east out of La Paz Bay, round the corner and head south, the first decent-sized island you'll come to is Isla Ceralvo. It takes longer to get to than Isla Espiritú Santa (it's about a 1 1/2 to 2 hour boat ride in a double engine Super Panga from La Paz — and about the same from Buena Vista as well) but the diving is said to be spectacular.

The snapper (or huachinango, if you recall, in Spanish) is another one of those fish I caught lots of off the coast of La Paz during those Easter Vacations from ages nine to twelve.

And Isla Ceralvo was one of the islands we visited back then.

This is one of my sister's all-time favorite recipes and one she pilfered from a restaurant hanging out over the edge of the Sea of Cortez near Los Barriles. According to Nina, the delicate flavor of cinnamon and chile complements the fish wonderfully in this recipe. Why do people love it so? Well — the answer to that one is probably summed up in one word — taco. Yes, the snapper is seasoned first, grilled and served in soft tacos with avocado, onion and orange. A real palate pleaser. Serves six.

6 red snapper fillets, about 3 pounds
1 tbsp American chili powder
1 tsp cinnamon
1/4 tsp ground pepper
1 1/2 tsp salt
1/2 tsp oregano
1/4 tsp cayenne pepper
2 - 3 tbsp minced garlic
1/4 cup orange juice
1 tbsp grapefruit juice
1 tbsp olive oil
1 dozen corn tortillas
2 avocados, sliced
1 onion, minced
1 tomato, diced
1 orange, membrane removed and diced

Blend chili powder, spices and orange and grapefruit juices until a smooth paste is made. Spread paste over the fillets, top and bottom and set them aside to season overnight.

Brush the fillets with oil and barbecue for ten minutes on a side over the grill. Serve with hot tortillas and allow guests to make soft tacos with avocado, onion, tomato and orange.

RESTAURANT LA BUFADORA'S ORPHAN CALAMARI

Miguel Toscano (son of our patron, Señor José León Toscano) runs the La Bufadora Restaurant. When I asked him what his house specialty was, he told me, "Orphan Calamari." I didn't get it. "It's so delicious that in Spanish we say it needs no parent," he explained. I was still confused. Finally, he told me that a good translation for orphan in this sense would be, "outasite." Okay — I got it — Outasite Calamari.

After he gave me the recipe, he led me into the kitchen where his chef, Ricardo Vazquez, prepared two orders for us. As I watched, I scribbled like crazy. Afterwards, the guy I was with scarfed both of our servings down. He asked me to tell you that it's every bit as good as Miguel claimed it is. In fact, it's now both Derek's and Nina's favorite dish at La Buf Restaurant. Here it is for your dining pleasure. Like Ricardo, you can serve it with beans, rice and a Teaque Slaw or you can dress it up any way you like. It's not difficult to make, it serves six and it will earn you the reputation as a bona fide Baja chef.

6 calamari steaks
1/2 cup flour
3 cloves garlic, finely minced
2 eggs, beaten
salt and pepper to taste
1 - 3 tsp Tabasco or other red pepper sauce
1/4 cup milk
1/2 cup corn flake crumbs
2 tbsp butter or margarine
2 tbsp corn or canola oil
Ricardo's Outasite Orphan Sauce:
1/2 cup shrimp consomme
1 tbsp butter or margarine
1 cup milk

La Paz Sunset

© Bob Bonn 1997

2 tbsp brandy
3 tbsp parsley, finely chopped
1 red bell pepper, finely chopped
2 to 3 pinches flour, as needed
to thicken sauce

Partially defrost the calamari steaks. Using a knife, peel off the membrane surrounding the flesh. Put steak in a plastic bag, lay on a cutting board and pound until almost lacy. Repeat. Dredge steaks in flour. Season eggs with salt, pepper and red pepper sauce. Add milk to egg mixture. Dip calamari into eggs, then dredge again, in corn flake crumbs. Heat butter with oil in skillet until melted. Add garlic and calamari steaks and cook until golden on both sides. Place in oven to keep warm.

In another skillet, mix together all ingredients for sauce, stirring constantly. Add flour and thicken to desired consistency. Spoon over calamari steaks and enjoy!

PALAPA AZUL'S STUFFED CLAMS ON THE GRILL

The Palapa Azul is one of two restaurants at the end of the paved road on Tecolote Beach. To the north is an expanse of aquamarine water, merging with the darker blue water as one's eyes edge out towards Espiritú Santa Island. It's quiet there, unless the restaurant's generator is running so that the stereo can play Mexican country music. The restaurant is built into and around an old wooden fishing boat. The palm-thatched palapa roof leans off it and angles down towards the sea. All tables and chairs are planted right on the sand. You can take a swim and eat lunch in your wet bathing suit. You can catch a boat ride to the island and snorkel, dive or visit with the sea lions. And eat lunch when you get back. If you catch a fish while you're out, they'll cook it right up for you.

Nina and I swam in the 85 degree pale green water. Then we ordered lunch. Nina had this dish and the waiter shared the recipe with us. We're glad he did, because she swears it's way better than the stuffed clams she's had in much fancier restaurants in other parts of Baja — places where you have to wear shoes and that sort of thing!

These clams are served inside the shell, so you'll have to find a seafood market that sells them that way. Or else visit San Quintín, a few hours south of Ensenada and go clamming yourself. Or you could go to La Paz and dig them out of the bay there. Or Pismo Beach in central California. Or — the fish market! Whatever works for you! Just try it. It's a true Baja Lover's delight. Serves four.

16 chocolate or queen clams in their shells (about the size of your palm)
4 tbsp butter
6 - 12 fresh jalapeños, finely diced
2 cups Cheddar cheese, cut into small cubes
2 large white onions, finely diced
2 large tomatoes, finely diced
1 tsp garlic powder
2 Mexican limes, quartered
1 cup ham, finely diced
salt and pepper to taste

Remove the clams from their shells and dice into small pieces. Mix together in bowl with jalapeños, cheese, onion, tomatoes, garlic powder, lime juice and ham. Add salt and pepper to taste and scoop back into each of the 16 clam shells. Wrap each shell in aluminum foil and place over hot coals on the grill. Cook four minutes on each side. Nina recommends serving this with with beans, rice and Mexican Medley Chopped Salad.

CHICKEN, TURKEY, BEEF & PORK ENTREES

Tijuana Taxi

Remember the 80's? That decade not so long ago when the Baby Boomers transformed themselves from latter day hippies (many of whom had indeed inhaled) into serious, ladder-climbing yuppies? When conspicuous consumption was in and our credit card bills escalated right along with the national debt?

debt? When comparing ourselves to our neighbors and friends was epidemic? And when Corporate America was considered the only place to find our identity, security and value?

I was the consummate upwardly mobile urban professional in those days — so slick and so thirty-something! Everything and everyone had a label. My friends and I became as obsessed with labels as we did with health and fitness. We were as hooked on our images as we were on aerobics, light mayonnaise and a whole plethora of fat-reduced or fat-free foods. By the end of the decade even nine year olds could quote the number of fat grams in a granola bar.

My how things have changed. Now that most of us have had our lives downsized — either by the economy, corporate restructuring, divorce, or all of the above — we've been forced to look at ourselves in the mirror, rip off the labels we thought defined us and try to figure out who we really are and just what the heck really matters in life. I have learned, that riches are fleeting and beauty fades — eventually. Hopefully, I've learned to love others more, not squashing them like bugs as I clamber to reach that pot of gold at the end of some rainbow.

That's why I went back to Baja — back to simple, humble, rural Baja after my divorce ended the fancy Cabo and Puerto Vallarta vacations of the 80's. I needed to relearn things like trust, faith and love. Other things like adventure, laughter, hope and joy. And I did learn. I'm still learning and with God's grace I will never stop.

Think of this section on chicken, turkey, beef and pork entrees as a "Best of the 80's." Like all conscientious chefs, ten or so years ago, I set out on a mission to formulate recipes using only the healthiest ingredients. And of course, the healthiest meats were lean, leaner and leanest. I created some of these recipes after eating a wonderful dinner in an exotic restaurant. Others I got from friends and family members. I even found a few in magazines, tried them and adapted them to my particular Baja style of cooking.

My family and I still enjoy these dishes. Why? Because they taste good, they're fun to make and they're good for us too! Can you beat that?!

SNOWBIRD CHICKEN IN TOMATILLO SAUCE

I got this recipe from a Canadian Snowbird who was traveling in a caravan of 14 monster motor homes down Baja Highway 1. She was a burly 60ish widow lady from Calgary who was piloting her own ship, so to speak. Feisty, hard-drinking and full of raucous stories, her group camped next to ours on a previously secluded (until the Snowbirds showed up and took it over!) beach just to the south of Santa Rosalía. We cooked dinner together that night and it most certainly was a winner. Snowbird Chicken is a great dish with a true Baja flair, but it isn't spicy-hot, so you can comfortably try it on your more tentative friends. Serve it with Jicama Fresca as an appetizer, and with your dinner, if you want to really jazz things up, include Avocado Soup, Sinful Cinnamon Rice, and a Margarita Pie for dessert. Serve with a light, white wine like a Mount Xanic Chardonnay. Serves six.

12 filets of boneless skinless chicken breasts
2 cups water
1/2 pound canned tomatillos
1/2 bunch cilantro, stems removed and chopped
1 stalk celery, cut up
1 cup green onions, chopped
1 small bunch leaf lettuce
1/4 cup sunflower seeds
1 3 1/2 ounce can whole green chiles
1/4 tsp ground cumin
1/4 tsp garlic powder
1 tsp butter or margarine
salt to taste

Boil chicken for 25 minutes in water. Drain chicken, reserving broth. Keep chicken warm. Place half of tomatillos, cilantro, celery, green onions, lettuce, sunflower seeds and chiles in blender. Add 3/4 cup broth and blend well. Repeat with remaining half of same ingredients plus 3/4 cup broth.

Combine, then blend in cumin and garlic powder. Heat butter in large skillet. Add tomatillo mixture and simmer 15 minutes over low heat, stirring until thickened. Add more chicken broth if sauce gets too thick. Season to taste with salt and serve hot over chicken.

CHILI CHICKEN WITH CITRUS GLAZE

This incredibly yummy dish is one my mom created with her friend Helen Chadwell on one of our family camping trips to Kilometer 181, a few hours south of Ensenada. We took a lot of trips together with the Chadwells when I was growing up. They loved Mexico and camping as much as we did and their sons, Brandon, Brent and Bryan were all close to Nina's and my ages. We got along famously and had some pretty amazing adventures together.

On this particular trip, the boys' paternal grandfather was along. My dad had just bought an old Scout, a four-wheel drive miniature pickup truck and we kids and the three men took off down some really bad roads in search of some really good places! We found them too. I remember a deserted beach with miles and miles of tide pools and really big waves where my dad and Ben and Ben's dad taught us how to surf fish. I remember running into a pair of young Mexican fishermen in their panga who'd beached their

boat and were free-diving in the chilly water. They kept coming up, again and again, with a lobster in each hand. Big lobsters. My dad and Ben bought a whole sack full and took them home for dinner.

That wasn't the night Mom and Helen made up this dish. But it was the same trip and you can bet there was a lot of feasting done — both nights! This chicken dish has a flavor hauntingly similar to a Mexican chicken mole. But it's much easier to make (think of it as a camping dish). I wrote down the recipe that night and since then, every time I serve it I get rave reviews. It's great with an Avocado-Tomato Salad and Los Cabos Chili Chips or with Sinful Cinnamon Rice and a Caesar Salad. Serves six.

12 filets of boneless skinless chicken breasts
1/2 cup American chili powder
1 tsp seasoned salt
3 tbsp butter or margarine
1/2 cup corn oil
3 tbsp orange marmalade
3 tbsp lime juice
2 - 3 tsp hot pepper sauce

Pound chicken breasts until tender. In shallow dish combine chili powder and seasoned salt. Coat each chicken breast with chili mixture. Set aside.

In large skillet, heat oil and butter or margarine over medium high heat. Cook the chicken breasts about five minutes on each side until browned and done. Remove chicken to plate. To drippings in skillet add marmalade, lime juice and hot sauce. Heat over medium heat, stirring to loosen crispy bits from bottom of skillet.

Return chicken to skillet. Cook two to three minutes longer until heated through and coated with glaze. Serve immediately.

CATAVIÑA CHICKEN ROLLS

I don't have the words in me to do justice to Cataviña. Cataviña is one of my ex-husband's sacred places. Midway between the Pacific and Sea of Cortez in the middle of the peninsula, a little less than a third of the way down, you can find it on a map due west of Gonzaga Bay. The Baja highway slices right through it, providing the traveler with stunning views of high country cacti found nowhere else in Baja, prehistoric rock formations and endless, endless blue sky. Aside from being the perfect place to stop overnight at the La Pinta Hotel on the way south, it is also a place to connect powerfully with the ancient Indian mystics who walked these hills so long ago.

I created this dish on a motor home trip back in the 80's. We were staying overnight at the one campground (which consisted of a dirt lot surrounded by a fence) in Cataviña on our way to the Bay of L.A. I was trying to make a Baja version of that great Russian entree, Chicken Kiev. I made it from ingredients I had on hand in my cupboards, and we were so impressed with how it turned out that we named it after our stopping place, Cataviña. Try with Aunt Hope's First Night in Camp Cole Slaw, some piping hot tortillas with butter and the dessert of your choice. Serves six.

12 filets of boneless skinless chicken breasts
1 1/2 7 ounce cans diced green chiles
6 ounces Monterey Jack cheese, cut in 12 strips
3/4 cup cornflake crumbs
1/2 cup grated Parmesan cheese

2 tbsp American chili powder
3/4 tsp salt
1/2 tsp ground cumin
1/2 tsp black pepper
8 tbsp melted butter or margarine

Sauce:
1 16 ounce can Mexican stewed
tomatoes, pureed
3/4 tsp ground cumin
1/2 cup green onions, chopped
salt, pepper and hot pepper sauce
to taste

Pound chicken pieces to about 1/4 inch thickness. Put about two tablespoons chiles and one strip Jack cheese in center of each chicken piece. Roll up and tuck ends under. Combine cornflake crumbs, Parmesan cheese, chili powder, salt, cumin and pepper. Dip each chicken in shallow dish of butter and roll in crumb mixture. Place chicken rolls, seam side down in oblong baking dish and drizzle with leftover butter. Cover and chill four hours or overnight. Bake uncovered at 400 degrees for 20 minutes.

To make sauce, combine stewed tomatoes, cumin and green onions in small saucepan. Season to taste with salt, pepper and hot pepper sauce. Heat well and spoon over chicken to serve.

TRIPÚI CHICKEN IN CILANTRO SAUCE

Seventeen miles south of Loreto, on Puerto Escondido is the Tripúi Trailer Park. Considered possibly the best in all of Baja, the park is under French ownership and management. It boasts an excellent continental restaurant, top-notch facilities and a nearly-completed marina. This light and ultra-simple chicken dish was created during a quick stop-over near Tripúi. This recipe uses the distinct flavor of cilantro to great advantage. You'll love it. Try it with a Wilted Cabbage Salad and some Caribbean Frijoles Negros. If you're in the mood for dessert, give the Pineapple Sopapillas a whirl. You'll definitely find yourself in elegant but casual mode — seated barefoot on a tiled patio with a stunning view of the ocean. Serves six.

12 filets of boneless skinless chicken breasts
2 tsp oregano
1 1/2 tbsp garlic salt
2 tsp black pepper
3 tbsp red wine vinegar
4 tbsp corn or canola oil
1 large onion, chopped

Cilantro Sauce:
1 bunch cilantro, stems removed
1 large onion, quartered
3 tomatoes, quartered
1 green bell pepper or 1 Anahem chile, seeded and quartered
1 - 2 hot yellow guero chiles, seeded

Marinate chicken breasts in mixture of oregano, garlic salt, pepper and vinegar. Heat oil in skillet, add chopped onion and cook until translucent.

Combine cilantro, quartered onion, tomatoes, green pepper and chile in food processor and blend until smooth. Add mixture to sauteed onions in skillet and cook two minutes. Add chicken pieces. Cover with water and simmer until chicken is tender, about 30 minutes.

SESAME-CHILI CHICKEN

Toasted sesame seeds, pumpkin seeds and spices give an almost Thai-type peanut taste to this unusual chicken dish. The chef who first prepared this dish for me at a long defunct restaurant in San Jose del Cabo had recently moved there from the incredible Caribbean diving resort of Cozumel. When I complemented him on it, he claimed that the sauce had its origins deep in the jungles of the Yucatán, way back in the days of the Mayans. I believed him, and you will too. It's definitely exotic, unusual and a treat for the taste buds! I recommend serving it with Gazpacho Blanco and Papas Fritas con Chile Verde. Serves six.

12 filets of boneless, skinless chicken breasts
4 tbsp sesame seeds
3/4 cup unsalted shelled pumpkin seeds (pepitas) or sunflower seeds if unavailable
2 cloves garlic, minced
3 tbsp corn or canola oil
1/2 tsp ground cinnamon
1/4 tsp ground cloves
1 tsp American chili powder
3/4 cup chicken bouillon
2 tbsp lime juice
1/2 head lettuce, shredded
1/2 cup sliced green onions
1 Mexican lime, cut into 6 wedges

Combine sesame and pumpkin seeds, garlic and oil in skillet. Stir over medium heat until sesame seeds turn pale golden brown. Remove from heat and add cinnamon, cloves and chili powder. In food processor, puree mixture until smooth, adding bouillon a little at a time.

Heat sauce over medium heat, stirring, until it begins to bubble and thicken. You can cover and refrigerate sauce for several days.

Bake chicken breasts at 350 degrees for twenty-five minutes. Heat sauce and add lime juice, stirring constantly until hot. Spoon over hot chicken, surround with lettuce and garnish with onion and lime wedges. Squeeze lime over chicken to taste.

ANITA-CONCHITA'S CHICKEN MOLE

The use of chocolate in the sauce makes this typical Mexican chicken dish unique. I tasted Mole (pronounced Moe-LAY) for the first time on a weekend trip to Ensenada when I was in grade school. Because of the dark, almost black color, I thought it was pretty weird back then. But as I grew older, I began to appreciate the subtle, multi-faceted and unexpected flavor of the chocolate. I would look forward to my first bite the way I looked forward to a swim on a really hot day. It's that good ....

Mole is a very special meal in Mexico, one that is served with tenderness to cherished loved ones. I was told this by the salesman, Ernesto, in a Cabo San Lucas store specializing in Huichol Indian art. These Indians live in the mountains behind Puerto Vallarta on mainland Mexico and have only recently begun to market their incredible, intricate works of art. This store had masks, suns, moons and wild animals like jaguars and wolves made exlcusively from tiny, multi-colored beads. Nina fell in love with an expensive sun and Ernesto offered it to her for considerably less — if I would go to a timeshare presentation (I didn't have to buy, he assured me — and I didn't) the next morning. He further bribed me by promising me his grandmother, Conchita's Mole recipe, (how could I pass that one by?!) which I've integrated into mine.

I've used boneless, skinless chicken breasts to make it less hearty and more suitable for today's eating styles. Why not serve it to someone(s) you love, accompanied by your favorites from some of the other sections of this book? If you prefer to use a prepared Mole sauce, I wholeheartedly recommend the sauce marketed by my friend, Mary Stec, owner of La Belleza Stoneground. You can buy her Stoneground Mole Negro or Stoneground Mole Coloradito, which have been made by the same Oxaxacan family in Mexico for over 200 years. Just call 888/639-2462. Or E-mail Mary for more information at LaBelleza1@aol.com. I first tasted her Mole Negro on a filet of beef at Restaurant Pancho's in Cabo San Lucas. And it was awesome. (Try it!) You will be amazed! Serves six.

12 filets of boneless, skinless chicken breasts
1/2 cup butter or margarine
1 onion, finely chopped
1/2 green pasilla, ancho or Anaheim chile, finely chopped
1/2 tsp pepper
4 cloves garlic, minced
1 17 1/2 ounce can tomato puree
1 1/2 cups beef bouillon
2 tbsp sugar
1 tsp American chili powder
1/4 tsp ground cinnamon
1/4 tsp ground nutmeg
1/4 tsp ground cloves
1 tsp sesame seeds
1 tbsp ground almonds
1 - 2 tsp hot pepper sauce
1 dark chocolate candy bar (about 4 ounces)
4 tbsp cold water with 2 tbsp corn starch

In large skillet, brown chicken slowly in butter. Remove chicken and add onion, bell pepper, pepper and garlic. Cook until tender. Add tomatoes, beef bouillon, sugar, chili powder, cinnamon, nutmeg, cloves, hot pepper sauce and chocolate. Add chicken, cover and reduce heat. Simmer until chicken is tender, about 50 minutes. Remove chicken to a serving platter and keep warm.

Slowly blend cold water into cornstarch. Pour into sauce and cook, stirring constantly until sauce is thickened. Spoon over chicken and serve.

POLLO LA BALANDRA

At the far end of La Paz Bay, just after you pass Pichilingue and the ferry docks and right before you get to Tecolote Beach is a famous rock formation known as La Balandra. It's shaped like a mushroom on a really long, skinny stem and it sits out in the light green water of a shallow bay right offshore. Accessible only by dirt road, it was actually knocked off its pedestal by vandals soon after the road was put through. Incredibly

enough, some local engineers got together and hoisted La Balandra back up onto its perch, where it stands majestically and precariously to this day.

This wonderful, delicate casserole dish of chicken with green chile was created on a camping trip on the beach closest to La Balandra, where there are a few ready-made campsites (meaning there are a few palapas scattered around on the deserted white sandy beach). You can swim or kayak from there out to see La Balandra for yourself before you have dinner. Be forewarned, however. Make enough! People are guaranteed to want seconds and it's easier than easy to make! How about serving it with Cantaloupe Soup Bahía Concepción and Mexican Rice? Serves six.

12 filets of boneless, skinless chicken breasts
salt and pepper to taste
1/4 cup butter or margarine
1/4 cup corn or canola oil
1 large onion, thinly sliced
4 7 ounce cans whole green chiles, cut in strips
1/2 tsp salt

2/3 cup milk
2 cups thick sour cream sauce
1/4 pound cheddar cheese, grated

Season chicken breasts with salt and pepper. Heat butter and oil together in skillet and saute the chicken filets for a minute on each side, until they're lightly browned. Set aside.

In same pan, fry onion until translucent. Set aside one can of green chiles. Add rest of chile strips to onions and cover. Cook over medium heat for five minutes. In food processor, blend reserved chiles until smooth with milk and salt. Add sour cream sauce and blend for a few seconds longer.

Arrange half the chicken filets in a 9 x 14 inch baking dish. Cover with half the chile strips and half the sauce. Repeat. Sprinkle cheese over the top and bake at 350 degrees for about 30 minutes, or until chicken is done and cheese is melted.

CHICKEN BREASTS WITH SANTA FE CHILE SAUCE

Another light, super easy winner, a favorite of Juan Carlos (cats do love chicken too, you know!) from the heart and soul of the Southwest. I swear you'll think you're in Santa Fe (or of course, as the gato keeps reminding me — Todos Santos!) if you serve this with Baja Cruiser Nachos as an appetizer, and Sinful Cinnamon Rice and Jicama Pico de Gallo. Serves six.

12 filets of boneless, skinless chicken breasts
2 cups Santa Fe Green Chile Salsa

Pound chicken breasts until 1/4 inch in thickness. Barbecue over grill while heating green chile salsa. Pour 1/3 cup of salsa over each two-filet serving.

PICHILINGUE CHICKEN IN NUT SAUCE

Next to the ferry dock on the east end of La Paz Bay is a lovely beach called Pichilingue. It has a restaurant and plenty of palapas on the beach to laze around under. On a trip my folks made with Aunt Hope and Uncle George some years ago, they had to wait several hours to catch the ferry to Mazatlán as it was running late for some reason or another. They decided to have lunch and go for a swim at Pichilingue.

My mom brought me this recipe back from there and encouraged me to try it. I did. The combination of the chipotle chile salsa, chicken, potatoes and almonds makes it truly unforgettable. It's another easy meal to prepare and one that will leave you hankering for a trip south. As a precaution, be advised that the chipotle salsa makes this dish fiery, so it isn't recommended for the more sensitive palates. Try it with Lentil Soup Borracho and a Chopped Mexican Medley Salad. Serves six.

12 filets of boneless, skinless chicken breasts
4 1/2 cups cubed potatoes
2 tbsp corn oil
2 cups salsa fresca
1 cup salsa chipotle
1 cup chicken bouillon
1 cup almonds, finely chopped
black olives for garnish

In large Dutch oven, brown chicken and potatoes in hot oil. Set aside. In saucepan, stir together salsas, chicken bouillon and almonds. Bring mixture to boiling. Pour hot mixture over chicken and potatoes. Bake, covered at 375 degrees for one hour. Garnish with black olives and serve.

MISSION TURKEY BREASTS WITH CHIPOTLE SALSA

Baja is rich in history from the Missionary Era, which began in the early 1500's and ended 300 years later when all the missions were secularized by the Mexican government. While Cortez, Ulloa, Vizcaíno and Cabrillo all explored the Magnificent Peninsula, it wasn't until Father Juan María Salvatierra, a Jesuit priest landed in Loreto in 1697 that a permanent settlement was established in Baja. The Jesuits built a total of 20 missions from 1697 - 1767 when they were expelled for abuse of authority.

At that point, Father Junipero Serra, a Franciscan , was assigned to care for the California mission system. He established only one mission in Baja before moving north to San Diego and Alta California. The Franciscans ceded the Baja missions to the Dominicans in 1773 and in the next six decades, the Dominicans built nine more mission in Baja. By then, however, the population of native Indians had shrunk (due to death by warfare and disease) to only a fraction of its original number, so there was no longer any economically feasible reason for the existence of the missions. By 1846 the era of the missions was over.

This dish is practically effortless to make. The aromatic, smokey flavor of the chipotle salsa complements turkey wonderfully. This entree is not for the timid, however! The chipotle chiles make it quite spicy. Try with a Caesar Salad and Chili Onion Rings and perhaps you'll be able to picture yourself sitting in a mission courtyard, shielded from the hot sun, eating your midday meal with the padres and the Indians. Serves six.

6 4 to 6 ounce turkey breast cutlets
salt and pepper to taste
1/2 cup flour
1 1/2 tbsp coarsely ground black pepper
6 tbsp butter or margarine
1 1/2 cups chipotle salsa (from the salsa section)

Pound turkey cutlets until 1/4 inch in thickness. Season with salt and pepper and lightly dust with flour.

Melt butter in skillet and saute turkey breasts for three to four minutes on each side, or until done. Heat salsa in saucepan until just boiling. Spoon over turkey breasts and serve.

CHICKEN ENSENADA

This delectable dish is named after Ensenada, busiest tourist town in all of Baja — which wraps itself around the grand bay of Todos Santos. Legend has it that the Spanish padres who first discovered Ensenada sat by the fire brainstorming one night, trying to come up with a name for the bay. They went through one saint's name after another, before finally throwing up their hands and just naming it after all the saints! It was simply too big and too impressive to hang a single saint's name on! The majestic bay extends from El Mirador on the north to Punta Banda on the south and it's a bustling seaport, the busiest on the west coast of Baja. We travel all the way through Ensenada and around Bahía Todos Santos on our way to La Bufadora, and so see it from every vantage point.

In the winter and early spring, grey whales and their calves frolic in its waters. My children witnessed the site of the season one year driving home from La Buf. They saw a huge grey throw itself up into the air, breach and then slam its mammoth body back down into the water. They oohed and aahed about it for weeks! Where was I? I was driving. I missed it completely.

Chicken Ensenada is similar to a Russian Chicken Kiev with a Chile Con Queso sauce. I tasted it first at a now defunct Baja bar and grill in downtown Ensenada and couldn't wait to get a chance to experiment with making it. It's wonderful served with Vegetable Kebabs, Jalapeño Corn Bread and a crisp salad. Serves six.

12 filets of skinless boneless chicken breasts
1 7 ounce can diced green chiles
1 7 ounce can sliced black olives
1 cup red bell pepper, finely diced and microwaved one minute
garlic powder to taste
salt and pepper to taste
3 cups Chile Con Queso (from Appetizer section)

Pound chicken breast filets until 1/4 inch in thickness. Put one teaspoon each of diced green chiles, black olives and red pepper inside each filet. Season to taste with garlic powder, salt and pepper. Roll and place seam-side down in greased baking dish.

Bake at 325 degrees for twenty minutes. Meanwhile, prepare Chile Con Queso according to recipe. When chicken is done, spoon sauce over the top of each filet and serve immediately.

FLANK STEAK SAN IGNACIO

This is dinner party material. If you have someone special coming to dinner, serve Flank Steak San Ignacio (named by my former husband and I on a trip to the exquisite mission town midway in the peninsula, between Guerrero Negro on the northwest and Santa Rosalía on the southeast). Even though San Ignacio isn't on the ocean, there's much to see and do. First of all, there's the Jesuit mission to visit. It is possibly the most beautiful in all of Baja. There are hundreds of prehistoric cave paintings in the nearby mountains.

Thirty miles southwest is San Ignacio Lagoon, one of the premier whale-watching destinations in the world. From November through March, here and in Scammon's Lagoon (to the north by Guerrero Negro) eco-tourists flock to visit with the grey whales (up close and personal) and to frolic with them and their newborn calves.

If you ever have the opportunity to take a trip to see the grey whales, do it. You'll never ever forget it! Another interesting place to visit near San Ignacio is Malarrimo Beach. Because the prevailing currents of the North Pacific all converge on it, Malarrimo catches flotsam and jetsam from all over the place. People have found World War II ration cans, redwood logs, even life preservers from Japanese boats. Malarrimo is windy and pretty hard to get to — but if you're a serious beachcomber, it's a place you don't want to miss!

Try this dish, inspired by our trip to San Ignacio, with Gazpacho Rojo, Marinated Vegetable Salad, hot buttered bolillos and your favorite hearty burgundy wine. The recipe sounds complicated, but it's much easier than it appears. And you won't believe how good it is. It'll be a hit — I promise. Serves six.

1/4 cup olive oil
1/4 cup red wine or Balsamic vinegar
6 cloves garlic, finely minced
2 tbsp cilantro, chopped
salt and pepper to taste
1 1/2 pounds flank steak, butter-
flied (sliced lengthwise
   through the middle of the steak,
leaving a hinge at far end)
1 red bell pepper
1 yellow bell pepper
3 tbsp cilantro, chopped
1 cup Chihuahua or Jack cheese,
grated
1/2 cup fresh basil leaves, chopped
salt and pepper to taste
cilantro sprigs for garnish

Make a marinade for the meat by combining olive oil, vinegar, garlic, cilantro, salt and pepper in a bowl. Add steak and marinade for two hours at room temperature or in the refrigerator overnight.

Halve the bell peppers, remove stems and seeds and place in a shallow baking dish. Bake at 400 degrees for 20 minutes until thoroughly softened. Puree bell peppers in food processor and combine with cilantro, cheese and basil in bowl. Set aside.

Lay marinated steak on counter top with flap opened. Spread pepper-cheese mixture evenly over both halves of the steak. Roll the steak up tightly, like a jelly roll and place seam down, in baking dish. Pour remaining marinade over steak.

Bake at 350 degrees for 30 minutes, basting occasionally. After removing from oven, let rest a few minutes before cutting into 1/2 inch slices. Garnish with cilantro sprigs.

ROSARITO RIBS DE FIERO

Straight from Rosarito Beach — party haven for college students from all over Southern California — and located just fifteen minutes south of the international border, come these spicy, delectable ribs. When I was newly single, the furthest south I dared venture on my lonesome was to Rosarito. I first tried these ribs at a roadside eatery claiming to specialize in carnitas. Carnitas? Can you figure that one out? I couldn't — so I asked. The proprietor told me that when they opened the restaurant their specialty was carnitas. It was only later, after his mother-in-law passed on that he and his wife decided to change their specialty. They just hadn't gotten around to changing the name yet. The logic was pure Baja. Anyway, who cared what the sign said?! The ribs were awesome. I told him so and he was so delighted, he gave me the recipe.

A few interesting tidbits of trivia regarding Rosarito. It became a destination for Hollywood celebrities fleeing Prohibition in 1927 when the famous Rosarito Beach Hotel was opened. The city has grown steadily over this century as nowadays decorators from the U.S. flock there to buy authentic, rustic Mexican furniture, such as the leather and wood equipales, its pottery, its folk art. It's a well-known surfing mecca and the site of the Rosarito - Ensenada 50-Mile Fun Bike Race, which attracts huge crowds every September and April. Not too long ago, Hollywood revisited Rosarito in a major way. A huge movie studio called Popótla was built just south of town next to the ocean, changing not only the face of the landscape, but also transforming the economics of the region.

Caution is in order here. These ribs have quite a bite. Save them for your friends who adore spicy foods. Or else invite me over for dinner! Serve with Fideo Tecate and White Rice with Vegetables. Serves six.

7 pounds pork ribs (you can substitute 10 pounds beef ribs)
1 medium onion, finely chopped
2 cloves minced garlic
1 tbsp butter or margarine
1 1/2 cups catsup
1/3 cup A-1 Sauce
3/4 cup honey
1 tbsp Worcestershire sauce
1 can beer
1 tbsp seasoned salt
as much Tabasco or other hot pepper sauce as you can handle
1 - 4 tsp New Mexico chile powder (or cayenne pepper)

Boil ribs in water for one hour. Meanwhile, saute onion and garlic lightly in butter. Add catsup, A-1 sauce, honey, Worcestershire, beer, seasoned salt, hot pepper sauce and chile powder. Bring to boil. Reduce heat and simmer 30 minutes.

Drain ribs and bake at 350 degrees 30 to 40 minutes or until brown, basting frequently with sauce during the last 15 minutes.

ALBONDIGAS EN CHIPOTLE

These meatballs are seasoned with spicy, smokey chipotle chiles. Originating as a country Mexican dish, this dish has become popular north of the border recently in the Baja Cuisine (that's the gringo name for fancy Mexican food) restaurant scene. Not overly hot, it deserves a try because the combination of flavors is truly spectacular. It's a robust meal that will warm up those cold, winter evenings. Try offering a Spanish Rice Salad Santiago with it, along with a platter of Special Quesadillas. (Is your mouth watering yet?) Serves six.

Meatballs:
3/4 pound ground pork
3/4 pound ground beef
2 small zucchinis, finely chopped
2 eggs
1/4 tsp oregano
1/2 tsp ground pepper
3/4 tsp salt
1/4 tsp ground cumin
1 small onion, chopped

Sauce:
6 - 8 tomatoes
3 - 5 chipotle chiles en adobo
3 tbsp corn or canola oil
3/4 cup chicken bouillon

To make meatballs, combine pork, beef and zucchini. In food processor, blend eggs, spices and onions. Mix well into meat and make 24 meatballs, about 1 1/2 inches in diameter.

Cover tomatoes with boiling water in Dutch oven and cook about five minutes. Drain. Skin tomatoes and blend with chiles to make a smooth sauce. Heat oil, add sauce and bring to boil over high heat. Cook for five minutes. Add chicken bouillon and reduce heat. Add meatballs, cover and simmer for 50 minutes or until meatballs are done.

CASA SALSIPUEDES FIFTEEN BEAN CHILI

We call our La Buaqdora house, "Casa Salsipuedes" because salsipuedes means, "get out if you can!" Like the Eagles have always reminded us in their song, "Hotel California," (the hotel really does exist — and it's in Baja — in the west cape town of

Todos Santos) once Baja Magic has you in its thrall, you can get your body out all right, but you'll never be able to get your soul to leave! I guarantee it.

This is my 100% original chili recipe. I swear it's as hot as any Texas chili, especially if you go heavy on the New Mexico chile powder or chipotles. I like it that way. While my claim to fame is that I use 15 different kinds of beans, my chili's intense heat has raised more furor among my dinner guests than its originality. I've seen many a friend's forehead break into a sweat over the years as they poured glass after glass of water down their blistered throats. (Well, maybe not quite that bad!)

Actually, I've learned over the years that I have to (no pun intended) cool it on the hot stuff. So, if like 99% of the world, you prefer your chili milder than I do, just leave out the New Mexico chiles. Or go light on the chipotles. Taste it as you go along, adding chiles very slowly.

During the winter months it gets cold and dark early in La Bufadora. When the only lights are solar (which tend to be both precious and dim), candles or propane lanterns (same principals apply here), and the only heat emanates from the fire place, we all tend to go to bed early. But a robust, tummy-warming dinner of Fifteen Bean Chili makes it a whole lot easier to bear the cold. After all, it is guaranteed to warm you from the inside out.

Whether you make it in Baja or in rural Tennessee, a pot will last you a few days. If you serve it up for a crowd, as long as you learn from my mistakes and keep it on the mellow side, you will be praised. I promise! Serves six to eight.

1 1/2 pounds lean ground beef
1 1/2 pounds smoked turkey sausage, ground
2 large onions, chopped
3 garlic cloves, minced
1 16 ounce bag "15 bean soup" (beans only)
1/4 cup American chili powder
New Mexico chile powder or chipotle chiles in adobo, pureed and to taste (optional)
1 tbsp salt
1 tsp pepper
2 1 pound 12 ounce can Italian tomatoes in puree
2 tbsp oregano
Garnish:
2 cups grated cheddar cheese and 1 chopped onion

Soak beans overnight according to directions on package. Drain and rinse thoroughly in collander. In Dutch oven, brown beef, pork, onion and garlic. Drain off excess fat. Add beans and all remaining ingredients and bring to boil over high heat. Reduce heat, cover and simmer for at least two hours or until beans are tender and all flavors well-blended. Serve in bowls and garnish with grated cheese and chopped onion. Add a dozen or so hot, buttered tortillas to round out the meal.

EXPATRIATE PEPPER STEAK

Another La Bufadora original, I dreamed this up over Christmas vacation and named it after my expatriate buddies, Jim and Sue. My pepper steak is slightly different from the cracked black peppercorn version you may be used to, but it's definitely tasty. The flavors of the cilantro, wine and mushrooms blend with the green peppercorns to make a subtly different but delectable sauce. Try it with a Caesar Salad, fresh Vegetable Kabob and a hearty red wine.

This makes a perfect holiday dinner. I remember when I first created it. I served it to a few friends (including the expatriate duo) on New Years Eve, before we went out to Los Gordos, one of our favorite local hangouts for their big new year's fiesta. Gayle, my daughter, got to stay up until midnight for the first time that year. Her favorite memory of the party was of hiding behind a tall, handsome hombre out on the patio at Gordos and watching all the caballeros (Mexican gentlemen — aka — cowboys) empty their six shooters into the New Year's sky as the moonlight flickered on Papalote Bay. Only in Mexico. And only in the boonies!

1/4 cup butter, margarine or corn oil
6 medium steaks
6 green onions, chopped
1/2 cup chopped cilantro
1/2 pound fresh mushrooms, sliced
1/4 cup green peppercorns
1/2 cup white wine
salt and freshly ground pepper to taste
lemon and tomato slices to garnish

Heat butter or oil in skillet. Fry steaks three minutes on each side and remove to hot platter. In remaining butter, add onions, cilantro, mushrooms, green peppercorns, wine, salt and pepper and cook until mushrooms are tender. Pour sauce over steaks. Garnish with lemon and tomato slices.

MEDALLIONS OF PORK MULEGE STYLE

We spent some time in Mulege when I was 11. This is what I remember from that trip: 1) The Audubon Society was in town. Famed author, Roger Tory Peterson was there and let me and Nina tag along on bird-watching expeditions at sunrise and sunset along the Río Mulege and through the hillsides. 2) We paid the bird-watchers back by performing a water ballet just for them in our hotel's pool. 3) Nina sat on a jumping cholla that trip and it took Mom over an hour to pluck out the nasty thorns. 4) We flew in and out in a friend's private plane. When we got ready to leave Mulege, the plane was so overloaded that the pilot had to abort take-off, go back and dump a bunch of weight. When we tried to take off the second time, it was a real white-knuckler according to our mom (who has flown with some real World War II hot shots in her time and isn't a fearful flyer by any stretch of the imagination). She said we came way close to stalling and barely cleared the mountain at the end of the runway. Fun trip!

The orange and wine flavors work feats of magic with the pork in this recipe, transforming it into an elegant entree. One of my swimming buddies goes to Mulege all the time. Since she knew I was a collector of unusual Baja recipes, she brought me this one back from a trip a few years ago. It will truly convince you that you are seated amid a palm grove along the river, in the exotic, tropical oasis of Mulege. Or at least you'll wish you were! Enjoy with Celia's Summer Nopales Salad, Rajas en Crema, piping hot bolillos and a chilled Sauvignon Blanc. Ah yes! Serves six.

3 pork tenderloins
2 tsp dry mustard
salt and freshly ground pepper to taste
2 tbsp butter or margarine
2 - 3 cloves garlic, minced
1/2 cup dry vermouth
1/2 cup dry white wine
1 cup orange juice
1 tbsp flour
2 tbsp water

Garnish:
cilantro sprigs
2 tbsp chopped cilantro
2 tbsp zests of orange rind
1 orange, sliced thinly

Trim fat and sinew from pork tenderloins and cut in 1/2 inch thick slices. Combine dry mustard, salt and pepper, and lightly rub into meat.

In large skillet, melt butter over medium-high heat. Add pork slices and garlic, browning for three to five minutes on each side. Add vermouth, wine and orange juice, and reduce heat. Simmer, covered for eight to ten minutes or until meat is tender. Remove medallions to warm plate and cover.

Make a paste of flour and water. With flat whisk, stir the paste into pan juices and simmer to thicken.

When ready to serve, return the medallions to the hot pan gravy for a minute, then arrange on a warmed serving platter. Cover with gravy. Sprinkle with chopped cilantro and zests of orange rind, placing sprigs of cilantro and slices of orange around platter.

RENEGADE ENTERPRISES

MEMBER OF

Small Publishers Association
of North America

© Bob Bonn 1997

Fat Cat Ranch

BREAKFAST & BRUNCH

Desert Java

We have a saying in La Bufadora that applies only to newcomers. It's called, "getting boofed." Exactly what *does* that mean? Let me give you a little background.

There are four restaurants on the main drag, which is next to a shopping arcade full of curio shops, folk art shops, taco stands and a fifth restaurant called "Los Panchos." There are stands that sell churros (long, skinny, deep fried donuts dipped in cinnamon sugar) and stands where you can buy fresh fruit in a cup or an an ear of corn smothered in butter, hot sauce and Mexican cheese. On Wednesdays, Fridays, Saturdays and Sundays this "mall," as we call it, swarms with tourists. They come in by the busloads from Ensenada to see La Bufadora, one of the biggest blow holes in the world. Local legend has it that the name means "Buffalo Snort," which is exactly the sound the water makes as it's sucked into an underground tunnel, a moment before it explodes from the rocks and bursts sky high, drenching onlookers.

Across Bahía Papalote (Kite Bay) is Toscano's ranch where our gringo colony of trailers and homes is located. People come to see the Blow Hole, but they don't spend the night. There are a few houses to rent in La Bufadora, but there are no hotels. Unless you know someone, or unless you're a diver who doesn't mind camping in the dirt, you never get any further than the touristy part of town. You come in, you shop, you eat, perhaps you stop into Gordo's for a shot of Rattlesnake Tequila, or you try one of the El Dorado's authentic Margaritas, or you have some nachos at Celia's. On your way out of town, you may decide to have chips and salsa with a Tecate beer at Restaurant La Bufadora. But you don't stay. (After all those drinks, perhaps you should!)

Nina is a diver. She found a house to rent and invited me and my kids to spend Memorial Day weekend in La Bufadora a few years back. We went. The first morning we were there, we all walked through Toscano's ranch to Gordo's. After all, breakfast was advertised for $1.50 so how could we go wrong? I ran into an old friend from San Diego on the patio there and he invited us on up. As we sat on the deck in the early morning sunlight, my eyes drifted out over the bay. It was beautiful, peaceful, festive, lonely, comforting and magical. My heart stirred, my eyes misted up and in an inexplicable way, I felt I'd come home. Home to somewhere I'd never been before. Bingo. I was boofed. What happened to me?! I can only tell you that it reminded me of the Baja I'd come to love as a kid — and almost forgotten existed in the intervening decades!

I stayed an extra night that trip. I came back again, again and again that summer. I couldn't stay away. I was growing there — happy there — free there — me there. Nina and I ended up buying a house there after the summer passed. I dedicate this section of my cookbook to being boofed. Whether it happens to you in

La Bufadora or somewhere else in Baja, it's when the magic of the place zaps you, captures you, sits you right down and makes you its own. You become a part of it and it a part of you.

HUEVOS RANCHEROS

Huevos Rancheros, or eggs ranchero style are a traditional Mexican breakfast. You can get them in the restaurants at La Bufadora for under two bucks each. You can get them in just about any restaurant anywhere in Baja that serves breakfast, actually! They're terrific with frijoles, buttered tortillas and fresh fruit and perhaps a round of Bloody Marys if you're so inclined. Serves four.

8 eggs
4 tbsp butter or margarine
salt and pepper to taste
8 corn tortillas
1/2 cup corn or canola oil
4 cups Pancho Villa's Salsa Ranchera
2 cups Chihuahua or Jack cheese, grated

Fry eggs in butter in skillet while heating salsa in a sauce pan. Season to taste with salt and pepper. Fry tortillas flat in corn oil in small skillet. Drain on paper towels. Place one fried egg on each tortilla. Top with salsa and grated cheese. Place under broiler for one minute or until cheese is melted. Serve immediately.

ANN'S HOT-CHA-CHA OMELETTE

My friends, Larry and Hal owned a restaurant years ago in Encinitas, CA. They made the best omelette I had ever eaten, but I had a little complaint. There wasn't any hot sauce to go with it, what with their food falling into the California Cuisine category and all. So what did I do? I brought a bottle of Huichol Hot Sauce with me in my purse one Mother's Day for brunch. Hal told me he was renaming the omelette in my honor. (Of course, it was just a joke, but I took him up on it here!) Believe me, the only thing that's hot is the sauce. Everything else is still as Larry conjured it up back then — and it's purely divine. Try it with fresh fruit, Papas Fritas con Chile Verde and coffee for a casual but elegant brunch worthy of Larry and Hal. Serves four to six.

1 dozen eggs, lightly beaten
1/3 cup milk or half and half
1 tbsp garlic powder
salt and pepper to taste
1/2 cup butter or margarine
2 avocados, peeled and thinly sliced
8 slices bacon, cooked and drained
2 cups Chihuahua, Jack Muenster or
Brie cheese, (or a combination
thereof) crumbled
1 tbsp American chili powder to
sprinkle on as garnish
salsa fresca or hot pepper sauce to
taste (if desired)

Beat eggs with half and half or milk.
Add garlic powder, salt and pepper.
Heat an omelette pan to medium
heat. Melt one fourth of the butter
or margarine to cover the bottom of
the pan.

Pour one fourth of the egg mixture
into the pan and cook until lightly
browned on bottom, about two minutes. Add half an avocado, sliced,
two slices of bacon and half a cup of
grated cheese. Cover pan and continue heating until cheese is melted.
Fold omelette in half, garnish with
chile powder and serve immediately.
Serve plenty of salsa on the side for
those who desire it.

CABO BAJA OMELETTE

One of my all-time favorite Mommy
Memories is of the first time I took
Gayle snorkeling in Chileno Bay. We
sneaked out before breakfast and
dove into the warm water right after
the sunrise. We held hands as we
kicked through schools of yellow and
grey striped tiger fish, spiny brown
spotted blow fish and rainbow-colored
parrot fish. "Umph, umph!" we'd grunt
through our mouth-pieces as we
pointed to the reef below. I remember
diving. Seaweed waved at me. Fish
stared and swerved from my path.
My ears crackled. I swam on, searching
the cracks between rocks for those
devious, darting flashes of fluores-
cent blue, yellow and turquoise —
those tiny, exotic tropical sea creatures that are the most spectacular
of all. Moments before my air ran out, I
found two. Turned towards the surface and pointed. I heard Gayle's
water-muffled laughter as the fish
burst forth to gleam briefly in the rip-
ples of reflected sunlight.

When she got tired, we caught a gen-
tle wave that beached us at the
shoreline. We took off our snorkels and
sat together as the waves lapped at

our legs. Then we walked down the beach. I told her stories from my childhood, about this land of endless uninhabited coastline, simple folk and incomparable majesty.

I remember seeing it through her eyes, as though for the first time. It was my favorite time of year in Southern Baja — October. The usually barren landscape was alive with color. There had been an inordinate amount of rain and the hillsides to our back were covered with wild California red bougainvillea. Flowering shrubs twined themselves seductively around the tall, many-armed cardon cacti. Stocky, over-built elephant trees lounged next to orange-blossomed, lush-leafed ocotillos. The desert had been transformed into a tropical thorn forest of jungle greens, perfumed with fragrant crimson, yellow and purple blossoms. We passed a washed out river bed. Whenever the rains unloaded on the mountains behind us, the waters would race to meet the sea, ripping up vegetation and tossing the debris of the hillsides on these now tranquil shores.

Her growling stomach turned us back around and we returned to the Hotel Cabo San Lucas for breakfast. This recipe was inspired by that magical Baja morning. It makes six two-egg omelettes, but can serve four if you prefer three-egg omelettes. The fresh ingredients and fiery chiles make it a winner in my book. Try it with fresh fruit, hot bolillos, Caribbean Frijoles Negros and Sangría Blanca for a to-die-for brunch.

12 eggs, lightly beaten
1/3 cup milk or half and half
1 onion, finely diced
1/2 bunch cilantro, with stems removed and finely diced
2 tomatoes, diced
4 cloves garlic, minced
1 3 1/2 ounce can diced green chiles
1/4 to 1/2 cup diced jalapeños (optional)
salt and pepper to taste
2 cups Chihuahua or Jack cheese, grated
1/2 cup butter or margarine

Place diced onion in microwave cooking dish. Cook on high for two minutes, or until onions are wilted. Mix with cilantro, tomatoes, garlic, diced green chiles and jalapeños. Add salt and pepper to taste. Microwave again on high for an additional minute, or until all ingredients are hot.

Heat an omelette pan to medium

heat. Melt one fourth of the butter or margarine to cover the bottom of the pan. Pour one fourth of the egg mixture into the pan and cook until lightly browned on bottom, about two minutes. Add one fourth of the onion, cilantro, tomato mixture and one fourth of the cheese. Cover pan and continue heating until cheese is melted. Fold omelette in half and serve immediately.

QUESO FUNDIDO CON JAMÓN

In English we call this a puffy cheese bake. It is a rich and spectacular brunch entree I learned to make from a Mexican friend who lived in Tijuana and one I love to serve my extended family on Christmas morning. Offered with fresh Watermelon Fruit Salad and Bloody Marys (or just plain coffee) it will make you a proud chef whenever you serve it! Serves six.

8 slices sour dough bread, buttered
6 eggs
2 cups whipping cream
4 tbsp melted butter or margarine
1 tsp salt
1 tsp dry mustard
1/2 tsp paprika
cayenne pepper to taste

1/2 tsp paprika
cayenne pepper to taste
3 cups cheddar cheese, grated
3 cups ham, cut into chunks with fat removed

Butter a 9 x 14 dish. Line the bottom and sides of the baking dish with buttered bread. Beat eggs slightly and add all remaining ingredients. Mix well. Pour into baking dish and bake, uncovered at 350 degrees for 40 to 50 minutes or until cheese is bubbling and golden brown.

SUNRISE MACHACA CON HUEVOS

The tallest hill right on the coast at Buena Vista on the East Cape isn't all that tall. In fact, it only takes maybe twenty minutes to hike to the top of it. When you get there, you'll find a concrete monument that must be at least 100 feet high. Around it is a courtyard of sorts. A few years back, my kids and I got a collective bug in our bonnets and decided to get up before dawn and hike up there to watch the sunrise. Derek set his watch alarm for 5:15 and off we trucked. (It's a family secret that I wore my p.j.'s that morning, but no one would have known because they looked like shorts and a top!)

We got back in time for the fishermen's breakfast buffet. As we raved about our adventure in line to get our food, I happened to notice that a new friend of ours, an aerospace engineer named Steve who'd taken a real shine to Gayle and Derek was eavesdropping on us. Later on in the day, while playing water volley ball, he mentioned that he'd like to climb that hill himself and watch the sun swoop up over the Sea of Cortez. I laughed at him and said, "Hey, just show up at our door tomorrow morning at 5:15 and we'll do it again!" I didn't think anymore about it till the next morning at 5:15 when he came pounding on our door. And yes, we did stumble out again (only this time I didn't wear my p.j.s).

If you ever stay at the Buena Vista Beach Resort, by all means haul your heinie out of bed and go see the sunrise. It has the feeling of a sunset played backwards, because the sky lights up with wild red, orange and magentas which fade out as the burning ball of light slips up over the horizon and into the sky. If you do climb that hill, you'll get to see the town of Buena Vista come to life. You'll count upwards of 50 fishing boats bobbing quietly in the bay, waiting till all those gringos finish their breakfast and are ready to grab their poles and hit the decks!

This is a tried and true, quick and easy Mexican-style family breakfast from our fisherman's buffet line that can be served with a glass of orange juice and milk or coffee. Or add Frijoles, Wilted Cabbage Salad and Sopapillas for a great brunch. Serves eight — and hey, don't forget the salsa!

2 cups Shredded Beef (recipe in Tacos, Burritos & Tostadas section of this book)
8 eggs, lightly beaten
1/4 cup corn oil
1 onion, finely diced
1 to 1 1/2 cups salsa fresca
8 large flour tortillas

Heat the oil in a large skillet. Add shredded beef, eggs, onion and salsa. Cook until the eggs are done and all other ingredients are hot. Make burritos with the machaca by placing filling inside a flour tortilla, folding one end over and rolling. Place seam side down on plates. Serve immediately.

BAJA AH-HA BREAKFAST TACOS

Breakfast tacos could almost be considered the Border region's counterpart to French Toast. The tortillas are dipped in egg batter, fried and stuffed with all types of breakfast treats. You can vary the ingredients depending on your mood. Kids and adults alike will love helping you assemble and devour these.

And why do I call them Baja Ah-Ha Breakfast Tacos? Because my dad made them for me and Nina once when we were kids, camping on a lonely hillside at the edge of the Pacific. We'd already been out body surfing and shell hunting and it was past 8:00 AM and we were seriously hungry. The smell of those tacos assaulted our olfactories as we hiked up onto the bluff with our dog, Victoria. As you munch our stateside version, you'll be able to feel yourself barefoot on that isolated piece of Baja real estate, your toes crusted over lightly with golden dust and your hair damp from swimming. Imagine the sun easing up over the hills to the east, the coffee perking on the Coleman stove — and take your first bite. You'll be there!

Really. These Baja Ah-Ha Breakfast Tacos will definitely alter your perspective on the day. Serves six.

6 tbsp butter or margarine
6 corn tortillas
6 eggs
salt and pepper to taste
1 cup crumbled bacon (or 1 cup chopped ham or 1 cup crumbled sausage)
1 cup cheddar or Monterey jack cheese, grated
1 avocado, chopped and sprinkled with lime juice
1 3 1/2 ounce diced green chiles
1 large tomato, chopped
4 green onions, chopped
1 cup thick sour cream sauce
1 cup salsa fresca

Melt half the butter in an omelette pan over medium heat. In a medium sized bowl combine slightly beaten eggs, salt and pepper. Dip a corn tortilla in the egg batter and fry one side of the tortilla about 1/2 minute, or until golden brown.

Turn tortilla over and place bacon, ham or sausage, cheese, avocado, chiles, onions, tomatoes and a dollop of sour cream sauce inside the tortilla. Fold over and cook until cheese is melted. Repeat for all tortillas, adding the rest of the butter to pan as necessary. Serve with salsa on the side for those who wish it.

CHORIZO

No Baja cookbook would be complete without chorizo. It originated as a spicy Mexican sausage and has become an integral part of our regional cooking. It can be served as a breakfast sausage, can be added to potatoes, soups, eggs, tacos — just about anywhere you want to add a spicy, delicious, definitely Mexican sausage. This recipe makes about 4 cups and it's G-O-O-D !

1 large onion, finely chopped
6 cloves garlic, minced
1/2 pound lean ground beef
1 1/2 pounds lean ground pork
2 tbsp American chili powder
2 tsp oregano
3/4 tsp ground cumin
1/2 tsp cinnamon
1/2 tsp ground cloves
1 tsp salt
1 - 2 tsp hot pepper sauce
5 tbsp vinegar
1 1/2 cups enchilada sauce (use one of mine or canned sauce)

Combine onion, garlic, ground beef, ground pork, chili powder, oregano, cumin, cinnamon, cloves, salt, hot pepper sauce and vinegar.

In a large skillet, brown meat mixture lightly over medium-high heat. Break meat apart as it cooks. Add enchilada sauce and boil rapidly, uncovered, until liquid has cooked away. Skim off accumulated fat. Store, covered in refrigerator up to a week. Can be stored in freezer for much longer period.

CHORIZO QUICHE IN CORNMEAL CRUST

Imagine that you're sitting on the outdoor terrace of the famous, remote, fly-in (or drive-in via the rutted, washboard dirt road) just north of Los Barriles, Punta Pescadero. It's early morning and the sky is still rosy in the afterglow of sunrise. A flock of pelicans are gliding around the bay in front of you. More are perched on the rock formations jutting up out of the water. Every so often a bird spots his breakfast in the warm sea below and explodes downward into the water like a just-launched torpedo. A second later, Señor Pelícano pops back up to the surface, floating a moment duck-like as he scarfs down his meal. Then it's off to hunt again.

I've never (yet) stayed at Punta Pescadero overnight, but to me it's about the most romantic spot in all of Baja. A perfect honeymoon hideaway — a perfect romantic getaway period. The food and service are superb, the setting spectacular and the snorkeling, shell-hunting and beach and water sports are as good as they get. Anywhere.

This quiche was inspired by a brunch my family was invited to at Punta Pescadero one year. My mom and I couldn't wait to start experimenting when we got back to the States. The combination of the spicy chorizo, the eggs, cream and cornmeal make it an extraordinary regional delicacy. Try it with fresh fruit, a crisp Jicama, Orange and Red Onion Salad and champagne for an outrageous brunch. Or bring out a plate of piping hot bolillos and a frosty pitcher of Santo Tomás Sangria instead. Serves six.

6 slices Chihuahua or Jack cheese
1/2 cup cornmeal
3/4 cup sifted flour
1/2 tsp salt
1/8 tsp pepper
1/3 cup vegetable shortening
4 to 5 tbsp cold water
1/2 pound chorizo
1/2 cup green onions, chopped
4 eggs
2 cups whipping cream or half and half

salt and pepper to taste

To make cornmeal crust, sift together cornmeal, flour, salt and pepper. Cut in shortening until mixture develops texture of coarse crumbs. Add water, one tablespoon at a time, stirring lightly until mixture forms a ball. Turn out onto lightly floured board and roll dough to a 13 inch circle. Fit loosely into a 9 inch pie plate or quiche pan. Fold edge under and flute.

Place cheese slices on bottom of cornmeal crust. Fry chorizo until cooked and crumbly in skillet. Drain off fat. sprinkle chorizo on top of cheese, then top with green onions.

Lightly beat eggs in bowl. Stir in whipping cream, and season to taste with salt and pepper. Pour over cheese and chorizo mixture. Place on bottom rack of oven and bake at 450 degrees for 15 minutes. Reduce heat to 350 degrees and bake for 25 to 30 minutes longer. Let stand 10 minutes before cutting.

FR☺M THE BAR

© Bob Bonn 1997

Margaritas for Two

Have you heard those awful stories about folks who went to Baja, got rip-roaring drunk and ended up either sicker than a dog or in some kind of trouble? Well, I certainly have. And I've known a few of them folks in my lifetime. The summer before my senior year of high school, my parents had to bail a friend of mine out of jail, because he thought he had every right to bring his own beer into Hussong's Cantina in Ensenada. Not!

"Would you have done that in the U.S.?" my dad asked him the next day, right after he emerged from the Ensenada jail — filthy, frightened and exhausted. (Let me clue you in on something — he was only 19 and unable to even walk inside a bar stateside.) The rule of thumb I was raised by was to treat the Mexican people with respect — and — to behave as responsibly in Mexico as I do north of the border. I wrote that rule onto my heart. I've never gotten into trouble there.

Uh Oh. I just looked at the clock and it's 5:30. My guests will be arriving shortly. Time to finish the last minute preparations, put ice in the ice bucket and get ready for cocktail hour. What am I serving tonight? Margaritas? Nope. I'm not in the mood. How about Sangría? Red or White? No. Not Sangría either. Well, then, what about Renegade Rum Drinks? I don't know. I'm confused. Too many decisions.

"Hey, Nina! Help me decide something, will you please?" I holler into the living room. We pore over recipes and together we choose what we will serve this fine Baja evening.

You know, even though the following drinks (except Traditional Mexican Chocolate) are all cocktails, it's possible to create them without alcohol. I drank "Virgin Margaritas" and "Virgin Mary's" when I was pregnant. Both of my children are regulars at the swim-up bar at the Buena Vista Beach Resort. I can just see them now — gliding through the water, pulling themselves onto their submerged barstools and ordering in clear, confident voices: "Piña Coladas sin rum (without rum) por favor." Or, "Strawberry Margarita sin tequila."

Something I noted on a recent trip to La Paz, the cultural capital of Baja, as I was sitting in one of the countless sidewalk cafes that line its malecón, that coconut palm-crowned promenade that edges the bay was this: Mexicans are Latins. Like the French, Italians and Spanish, they consider the consumption of alcoholic beverages to be a natural part of life. When they drink, it's to celebrate life — but there's also a sacredness to the way they drink. Rarely does one see a drunken Mexican — more often, sadly — it's the gringos who overindulge and get out of hand.

Keep that in mind and you'll have great fun making, serving and imbibing in the drinks specified here. Margaritas were obviously created in Mexico, but they've been around so long they could easily be dubbed the California state drink. There are too many variations of Margaritas to offer them all here, but I've offered you a bunch. I've also included two types of Sangría, a wine, fruit and brandy-laced punch from Spain in this section, as well as recipes for home-made Kahlua and Irish Cream. And I've started the whole thing off with a lesson on tequila from John Bragg, the Maestro. What more could you ask?!

Oh. One last thing. What are you serving tonight?

THE TRUTH ABOUT TEQUILA

John Bragg has the largest collection of tequila in the world. At last count he had 247 different types of tequila, pulque and mezcal. Since 1990, he and his wife Mary have owned and managed Restaurant Pancho's (one of our all-time Baja favorites) in Cabo San Lucas. When we met them on a trip to Southern Baja not too long ago, Nina, John and I hit it off with both of them immediately. Mary fell in love with el gato, Juan Carlos (who was along for the ride) and she fell in love with this book too.

They invited us to dinner at their restaurant the next night and after we ate, John treated us to one of his Tequila Tastings. Because tequila is "the essence of Mexico," I think it's

only fitting that I should pass some of John's knowledge (which is as extensive as his collection) on to you. According to him, tequila isn't for light-weights — it's for those who, like the Mexicans, are passionate, strong and warm-hearted — people who live life with gusto. While most gringos think of tequila as something to be tossed back with a dash of salt and a lime, or added into a Margarita, serious tequila drinkers are thoughtful, slow sippers.

The Mayans started it all, way before the Spaniards showed up. Their fermented beverage of choice was pulque (pool-KAY) which they made from the Agave Mezcalero and used primarily for medicinal and religious purposes. In those days, drunkenness was a crime punishable by death and only old people and nursing mothers got free access to pulque. Why? Because of its high nutritional value and its tranquilizing effects. To this day, Indians still mix home-made pulque into their herbal medicines to treat diseases. And, as John told us, there are still pulquerías (pulque bars) in various parts of Mexico. He goes on to say that pulquerías generally don't have restrooms — just a trough on the floor in the back of the room — so they aren't for the faint-hearted! Or the ladies!

When the conquistadors and missionaries arrived in Mexico, they tried pulque, but at 30% alcohol, it just wasn't strong enough for their liking. So they did some experimenting and came up with Mezcal. Then they did some more experimenting with different varieties of agave and eventually came up with tequila. Tequila is made from the blue agave, or the Agave Tequilana Weber and is considered the most exceptional of all agaves because it produces the most full-bodied, clean tasting liquor. And it's all — every ounce of it — produced within 100 miles of Guadalajara. Today, over 90,000 acres of blue agave are being cultivated in this region, with the greatest number of fields near the small city of Tequila. About 45 miles northeast of Guadalajara, it's home to 20 distilleries (fábricas in Spanish) that produce over 55 million

duce over 55 million liters of tequila per year. Whew!

Most top-of-the-line tequilas are made from 100% pure blue agave. What does an agave look like, you ask? Well, it resembles a cactus with broad, flat leaves that come to a point on the end. When a plant is mature, at say, seven to ten years old, it shoots a flower-bearing stalk as high as 15 feet in the air. The dramatic yellow bloom will last a month or so, but it signals the agave's impending demise, for it dies soon after. Right before the stalk emerges is harvest time. Field workers remove the agave's core, called the piña, carry it to the fábrica where it's split in half and cooked in a large oven (or horno) for about 24 hours. After cooling another 24 hours, the piñas are crushed, strained, mixed with water and put in large vats to ferment. After fermenting for 72 to 150 hours, the liquid's filtered and put into stills. The distillation process is carried out twice, and the final product emerges at 100 to 120 proof. It's then diluted with distilled water until it reaches the proper range of 76 to 90 proof.

There are three types of tequila. The first is a blanco or joven. (HOE-ven, which means young) A joven is only aged one or two additional months. The second is a reposado (which means rested) which is aged in wood for three to 12 more months. John says, "A really good reposado grabs you by the throat and gently lets go." The third type of tequila, añejo (Ahn-YAY-hoe which means vintage) has been aged at least a year. Tequila ages quickly, so one that's five or six years old is considered, "muy añejo" or very old.

When we did our tasting, most of us preferred the blanco. John served us one called Don Juan and if you want to try your hand at some thoughtful, slow tequila sipping, this is definitely one to try. John has one parting thought he'd like to leave with you. If you come to Pancho's with a bottle of unopened tequila, and it's one he doesn't have in his collection, he'll buy the bottle from you and your dinner will be on the house! So, hey, that's worth a big Ole! Don't you think?!

REAL AUTHENTIC BAJA MARGARITAS

Easy, quick and always a hit, these Margaritas are the real thing. We have We have one rule in Baja. No mix. It just ain't the same! These are a great way to jump start any party. You can serve them on the rocks or blended, whichever way you prefer. Me — I like them both ways so I switch off. One blenderful serves four.

4 ounces tequila
4 ounces Mexican Controy (Cointreau or Triple Sec may be substituted)
juice from 10 - 12 Mexican limes, freshly squeezed
crushed ice to top of blender
Margarita salt (optional)

Place tequila, Controy, lime juice in blender. Fill until almost full with crushed ice. Shake well or blend until very slushy. Wet rim of martini or Margarita glass with water and swirl in small dish of salt. Pour Margarita into the glass. Ole!

WILD BLUE MARGARITAS from SOMEWHERES -VILLE

What?! Don't I mean Margaritaville? Probably. We play a lot of Jimmy Buffett music in La Bufadora. It fits the place. Like us Baja Aficionados,

Jimmy's a bit of an enigma. He hasn't had more than a couple of hits on the radio in his career (and no MTV videos), yet his concerts draw crowds that rank in the Top Five nationally. Never heard of a Parrot Head? Try buying a Buffett CD or two. You'll learn. And Jimmy's music will definitely adjust your internal compass — south. Try it. And try this Margarita — but don't forget your flip flops!

I semi-copied this un-copywrited (and thus don't claim it's a Buffett original) recipe, which serves two, off a t-shirt I bought at his Chameleon Caravan Concert in Del Mar, CA back in '93. This is more or less how it goes:

1. Fill shaker with broken ice —
2. Squeeze two fresh Mexican lime wedges into shaker —
3. Savor the fresh lime aroma —
4. Add two ounces of Cuervo 1800 or your favorite tequila —
5. Sniff the cork —
6. Add 1/2 ounce of Triple Sec —
7. Add 1/2 ounce of José Cuervo white tequila —
8. Add 1 1/4 ounces of Rose's Lime Juice —
9. Add a splash of Blue Curaco (Oh, baby!) —
10. Cover shaker tightly and SHAKE vigorously!
11. Flip shaker in midair (three times if you're a pro) —
12. Strain mixture over ice — kick back and turn up the tunes!

STRAWBERRY, PEACH or MANGO MARGARITAS

These totally tropical, spring or summer Margaritas are easy to make in your blender. Fun, tasty and refreshing, this recipe serves four and it's guaranteed to instantly transport you to somewhere south of the Tropic of Cancer! Serves four.

4 ounces tequila
2 ounces Mexican Controy
(Cointreau or Triple Sec may be substituted)
1 1/2 tbsp lime juice
1 1/2 cups fresh strawberries or 3 peaches (or mangos), pitted and peeled
crushed ice to top of blender
sugar (optional)

Put tequila, Controy, lime juice, and strawberries or peaches in blender. Fill to top with ice. Blend until very slushy and serve immediately.

If sugar-rimmed glasses are desired, wet top of martini or Margarita glass with water and swirl in small dish of sugar. Pour Margarita into the glass.

WINE MARGARITAS

Wine Margaritas are perfect for people who prefer a milder version of this potent drink. Restaurants around Southern California without hard liquor licenses invented them — for obvious reasons! The taste is still great, but without the kick of the tequila. Serves four.

6 ounces dry white wine
4 ounces Mexican Controy
(Cointreau or Triple Sec may be substituted)
the juice from 10 - 12 limes, freshly squeezed
crushed ice to top of blender
Margarita salt (optional)

Place wine, Controy and lime juice in blender. Fill until almost full with crushed ice. Blend until very slushy. If salt-rimmed glasses are desired, wet top of martini or Margarita glass with water and swirl in small dish of salt. Pour Margarita into the glass.

SANTO TOMÁS SANGRÍA

Sangría is a popular summer drink in Spain. It's fruity and tastes somewhat like a delicious wine punch. However, beware that the Mexican version has Controy and Brandy which give it an extra jolt.

This recipe makes a little over a gallon. Sangría may be served in tall glasses filled with crushed ice. It may also be served chilled in wine glasses without ice. Save the "drunk fruit" afterwards to use for a quick second batch if you run out, which you may — because it's really, really good! It is my signature drink and I named it after the Santo Tomás Valley just to the south of Ensenada in northern Baja, home of the famous Baja Santo Tomás Winery.

1/2 gallon burgundy wine
1 medium orange
4 cups orange juice
2/3 cup Mexican Controy, Cointreau or Triple Sec
1/2 cup brandy
1 apple
2 limes
1 pear
2 bananas

Using a vegetable peeler, peel the skin from the orange so that it's very thin. Put the orange peel in a small bowl. Using the back on a spoon, bruise the peel to extract the oil from the orange.

In a large punch bowl, combine wine, orange juice, Controy and brandy. Add orange peel and sugar into wine mixture.

Separate orange into sections and cut sections in half. Cut the apple and pear into small pieces, leaving the skin on. Half the limes and cut them into thin slices. Slice bananas. Add all fruits to wine mixture and chill at least four hours.

SANGRÍA BLANCA

Sangría Blanca is a lighter, less potent wine punch that could be best described as the "Los Cabos Sangría." Why? Well, since it's made with white wine, limeade, club soda and pineapple (instead of burgundy, brandy and the more hearty fruits), it's lighter and more tropical in its flavors. It's great for brunches or luncheons. This makes approximately one gallon and will transport you to those little latitudes!

1 6 ounce can frozen limeade
1 can water
16 - 20 ice cubes
1/2 gallon dry white wine, chilled
1 quart club soda, chilled
1 lime, thinly sliced
1/2 cup chunked fresh pineapple

Place limeade, water and ice cubes in blender and blend until slushy. Pour half mixture into each of two large pitchers. Pour half of the wine and half the club soda into each pitcher. Garnish chilled wine glasses with lime and a pineapple chunk. Serve immediately.

CHIMAYO COCKTAILS

The apple cider used in this authentic but little-known Mexican cocktail makes it a refreshing change from the typical Margarita. While seldom ordered by tourists, a perfectly chilled Chimayo Cocktail is a real treat to a Baja native — or an expatriated American who's been around a while! But beware — this is just as lethal as a Margarita, so take it easy! This recipe serves four, but if you want to try serving it as a punch, triple the amount of cider in relation to the tequila. It's an excellent, more mellow alternative.

12 ice cubes
5 ounces Cuervo Gold tequila
1 tbsp Creme de Cassis
1/2 cup apple cider
2 tbsp lemon juice
4 apple wedges for garnish

Fill a cocktail shaker with ice cubes. Add tequila, creme de cassis, cider and lemon juice. Shake well and strain into four glasses. Add the ice cubes and garnish each glass with an apple wedge.

LOS GORDOS
BLOODY MARYS

I like to call these "salad drinks," because whenever my friends and I find ourselves sipping them at sunset on the deck at Gordos in La Bufadora, we feel like we're doing something relatively healthy for our bodies. Believe us when we tell you — nobody, but nobody on planet Earth makes Bloody Marys as good as Chuy, the co-owner and bartender at Gordo's. You can try. I can try. But to really experience this drink, you have to try the real thing. At the real place. Made by the real guy.

On your first trip into Gordos, which is only open from noonish on Friday through noonish on Sunday — beware of locals who may try to entice you to drink a shot of Abel's famous (infamous?) Rattlesnake Tequila. (It's identical to the barrel at Pancho's in Cabo San Lucas) Well — one shot maybe. It's sort of an initiation rite. But if you get going on them, you may have a long, rather difficult night ahead of you! I recommend the Bloody Marys instead. Have one at sunset for me. Or — hey — have one with one of those $1.50 breakfasts. That's what boofed me, remember? Makes eight drinks.

Margarita salt
8 ounces vodka
1/2 gallon Clamato juice
10 limes
3 dashes Worcestershire sauce per glass
pepper to taste
hot pepper sauce to taste
3 sprinkles celery salt per glass
8 celery or carrot sticks for garnish

Rub the rims of eight highball glasses with lime and dip in Margarita salt. Fill glasses with ice and to each glass add: one ounce vodka, the juice of one lime, three dashes Worcestershire sauce, pepper, hot pepper sauce and three sprinkles of celery salt. Fill each glass to the brim with Clamato juice.

Garnish with celery or carrot sticks. Distribute among guests. Close your eyes, imagine yourself on Gordo's deck overlooking Papalote Bay and take a long swallow. Aaaaaaah ....

Wait a minute! Was that a pod of grey whales spouting off the end of Paplote Bay or did I just imagine that?! Nope. Thar she blows again! And wow, look at that calf spy-hopping! How cool! (See you at Gordo's)

SWIM-UP BAR PIÑA COLADAS

Have you heard Jimmy Buffett's song, "Margaritaville?" (Hasn't everyone?!) Does it remind you of hot, sodden days in tropical Mexico? Well — not me. The real scoop is that the tourists in La Paz, Los Cabos, Loreto and every other snazzy resort in Baja drink Piña Coladas. I know. I've hung out with them at enough swim-up bars

around the peninsula! Made from pineapple juice, coconut juice — and of course — rum, the flavor is pure tropics.

This blender-made version is less heavy and calorie-laden than Mexican Piña Coladas, but it's guaranteed to be just as delicious. Try these and you'll see yourself lounging under a palm tree next to the surf. Or on a submerged barstool in Buena Vista next to one of my kids (who drink them sin rum). Serves four.

6 ounces light rum
2 cups pineapple-coconut juice
(found in most grocery stores)
Ice to top of blender
Pineapple slices for garnish
dash of nutmeg

Pour rum and juice in blender. Fill to top with ice. Blend until very slushy. Pour into tall glasses and garnish with pineapple slices.

EAST CAPE COCONUT RUM COOLERS

In case you've forgotten, the East

Cape is one of the hottest up-and-coming resort areas in Baja. It extends from north of Los Barriles to Buena Vista and then south a ways to Cabo Pulmo. Its hub is located about 45 minutes north of the Los Cabos Airport.

The East Cape rightfully boasts that it has some of the world's greatest sport fishing. In fact, if you see bumper stickers around there that read "SUELTAME!" it means — "Release me." The area has an outstanding record for promoting conservation of its ocean wildlife through this catch and release program, which has kept lots of species (particularly the marlin and sailfish) off the endangered species list. Like I've said before, the East Cape also offers up great diving, wind surfing and any other kind of ocean sports you can imagine.

After a long day fishing or playing volley ball in the pool, order up one of these local delights and you will be amazed at how refreshed you'll feel! The combination of coconut rum, tonic, bitters and lime will delight your taste buds for sure — whether you're stateside sipping them in the back yard on a hot day or whether you're barefoot in Baja! This recipe serves four.

4 ounces light rum
4 ounces coconut rum (try Malibu or Captain Morgan's)
4 dashes of bitters
1 Mexican lime cut into quarters
tonic water
4 dashes fruit juice (any tropical punch/combination will do)
ice

Fill four tall glasses with ice. Add light rum, coconut rum and fill to the top with tonic. Put a dash of fruit juice and a dash of bitters in each glass and garnish with a slightly squeezed slice of lime. Serve immediately.

RUMBAS

From the Palapa Bar at the La Concha Hotel near the marina in La Paz come these light, tropical, fruity drinks. I first heard about them over the Internet. I was getting ready to make one last sweep through Southern Baja with Nina and John to scout up a few special recipes. I put up a notice on the Amigos de Baja web site bulletin board. One of the folks who responded encouraged me to try a Rumba (pronounced ROOM-bah) for myself and I did. It was good! And the waiter was kind enough to share the recipe with me. And now you gotta try one your-self — either there on the beach next to the Sea of Cortez just before sun-set like I did — or at home — like I will the next time. Serves four.

1/4 cup fresh papaya
1/4 cup fresh cantaloupe
3/4 cup pineapple juice
3/4 cup orange juice
6 ounces light rum
1 tbsp grenadine
ice
4 slices orange
4 maraschino cherries

Put all ingredients in blender and fill to nearly the top with ice. Blend until very slushy and pour into four glass-es. Garnish with orange slices and maraschino cherry on toothpicks, if desired. Or drink it plain, pure and simple.

RENEGADE RUM DRINKS

The first summer I spent in La Bufadora I hung out a lot with an old friend from San Diego named Kit. Having earned his living as a bartender for many years, Kit taught me how to make some killer rum drinks. I can still see his grin as I navigated the rather treacherous concrete stairs down to the beach at Papalote Bay, carrying a tray of umbrella, pineapple and orange-topped drinks in hot pink and blue plastic cups one late, late summer afternoon.

6 ounces rum
6 ounces cranberry juice
6 ounces peach juice or any other tropical juice
4 16 ounce neon plastic cups
ice
4 paper umbrellas
4 chunks fresh pineapple
4 slices orange

Fill cups with ice. Add rum, juices and stir. Top with pineapple chunks and orange slices skewered onto the paper umbrellas. Place on tray and serve outdoors with Jimmy Buffett music playing in the background. Serves four.

ROMPOPE

This drink can be found all over Baja and mainland Mexico in grocery and liquor stores. It's bright yellow in color, features a stunningly beautiful señori-ta on the label and is said to have been around for at least 600 years.

Supposedly, according to local legend it originated in northern Europe and found its way to Mexico with the padres. The Mexicans have since adopted it as their own and swear it cures colds and the flu, strengthens weak bones and even cheers up the elderly! While it's hard to adequately describe its rich, almost egg-noggy flavor, let me tell you that it's great with coffee after dinner or alone, on the rocks for dessert!

Here's a secret — this recipe makes approximately a gallon — and if you like it as much as the Baja natives do, you just might want to put it into some fancy glass bottles and give it away for Christmas presents. That's what we do.

2 quarts half and half
4 inches of vanilla bean or 2 tsp vanilla extract
2 cups egg yolks (about 2 dozen large eggs)
3 cups sugar
1 fifth of light rum

Heat half and half with sugar and vanilla bean until boiling. Immediately reduce heat and simmer for 20 to 30 minutes. Remove bean and cool.

In blender, beat rum and eggs for two minutes. Add milk and whip for another two minutes. Pour into bottles and chill. Will keep up to ten days in refrigerator. Serve warm or cold.

KAHLUA

This recipe allows you to make your own Kahlua. It is a traditional sweet, coffee-flavored Mexican liqueur, served most often as an after dinner drink. It can be served in a number of ways (recipes following). The recipe makes approximately half a gallon. If you're unsure about what to do with a gallon of Kahlua, consider doing what we've done with the Rompope and making it before the holiday season and putting it into small bottles to give as gifts to your friends.

2 cups water
4 cups granulated sugar
2 ounces instant coffee or decaf
1 quart 90 proof vodka
1 large vanilla bean

Boil water in medium sauce pan. Mix in sugar and coffee to water. Stir well and cool. Into half gallon bottle, pour vodka, sugar and coffee mixture and vanilla bean. Store for at least 30 days before serving or bottling as gifts.

EL DORADO ✦ ✦ ★
MEXICAN COFFEE

We locals call the El Dorado Restaurant in La Bufadora, "Fred's." Why? Because Fred is the owner. I specifically asked him for his Mexican Coffee recipe, because it is the best I've tasted anywhere. Truly. This piping hot drink combines the tastes of tequila, Kahlua, brandy and Rompope — all Mexican originals — with coffee. Topped with whipped cream, it is a dramatic way to end an evening.

Fred told me this coffee is best when flambeed, or served with a flaming sugar crust rimming the cup. I've never attempted flambeeing, and I don't recommend that you do either. It can be dangerous if you don't know what you're doing. I will tell you, however, if you ever get the chance to order one of these drinks down south at Fred's — I mean, the El Dorado — do it. It's incomparable. Serves four.

4 cups steaming coffee or decaf
2 ounces tequila
2 ounces Kahlua
2 ounces brandy
2 ounces Rompope (a creamy vanilla Mexican liqueur) or Irish Cream if unavailable
whipped cream to garnish

Heat four mugs by placing in hot water or heating in microwave. Into heated mugs, add half an ounce each of tequila, Kahlua, brandy and Rompope. Top off with hot coffee or decaf and whipped cream. Serve immediately in front of a roaring fire.

BLACK RUSSIANS
GUADALUPE

There are remnants of a turn-of-the-century Russian village (the original settlers were White Russians who ran to Mexico to escape the Communists) almost at the midpoint of the road that runs between Ensenada and Tecate in northern Baja, so there's no need to wonder how the Russians and Mexicans got together to concoct this drink. Kahlua and vodka are mixed together and served on the rocks. The taste is great, but the drink is strong. So beware. Serves four.

4 ounces vodka
4 ounces Kahlua
16 - 20 ice cubes

Fill four highball glasses to top with ice. Add one ounce each of vodka and Kahlua. Stir and serve immediately.

Mariachis

© Bob Bonn 1997

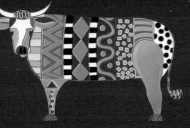

Five for Dinner

WHITE RUSSIANS

A less potent, but sumptuous member of the Russo-Mexican family of drinks, a White Russian is great when you're looking for something sweet and creamy — with vodka in it. Serves four.

4 ounces vodka
4 ounces Kahlua
2 cups milk or half and half
16 - 20 ice cubes

Fill tall glasses with ice. Add one ounce each of vodka and Kahlua. Add four ounces milk, stir and serve immediately.

KAHLUA AND CREAM

Rich, creamy and jammed full of calories and fat grams, Kahlua and Cream is a great after dinner drink for people who aren't counting. Serves four.

8 ounces Kahlua
2 cups whipping cream or half and half
16 - 20 ice cubes

Fill high ball glasses with ice. Add two ounces of Kahlua and four ounces cream to each glass. Stir and serve immediately.

ICE CREAM - KAHLUA ESPECIAL

This is truly what I would call a dessert drink. Serves six.

1 cup ice cold, strong coffee or decaf
1/2 cup vodka
1/2 cup Kahlua
1 quart vanilla ice cream or frozen yogurt
6 strawberries

Place half of the ingredients in blender. Blend only until ingredients are thoroughly mixed. Repeat. Serve in dessert bowls, garnished with strawberries.

CARLOS O'GRINGO'S MEXICAN - IRISH CREAM

You say there's no such thing as an Irish Mexican? Wanna bet?! Well, what about a gringo masquerading as an Irish Mexican?! Oh yeah, sure .... Only in Baja .... Only in Baja ....

For years, every Christmas I made gallons of Irish Cream. People requested it again and again, because they insisted that mine was at least as good as everyone's favorite big name brand! It can be put into small individual bottles and given as gifts, as I do. It's also great in coffee and in the other drinks which follow. This recipe makes a blender-ful, or about 5 cups and will keep in the refrigerator until the expiration date on the half and half.

2 cups brandy or whiskey
1 14 ounce can sweetened condensed milk
1 cup half and half
3 eggs
2 tbsp chocolate syrup
2 tsp instant coffee or decaf
1 tsp vanilla extract
1/2 tsp almond extract

Combine all ingredients in blender. Blend until smooth. Pour into bottles and store tightly covered in refrigerator for one month or until the expiration date on the carton of half and half. Shake well before serving.

IRISH - MEXICAN COFFEE

Irish Cream and tequila go hand in hand here to make a tasty coffee drink with a kick worthy of an Irish Mexican. Or a gringo masquerading as one. Serves four.

4 cups steaming coffee or decaf
4 ounces tequila
4 ounces Irish Cream
whipped cream to garnish

Into four mugs of steaming coffee, add an ounce each of tequila and Irish Cream. Top with whipped cream and serve immediately.

FROZEN IRISH CREAM

Frozen Irish Cream is my sister's and my creation. We invented it one Christmas Eve when my kids were tiny and spent the better part of the night drinking it while catching up on the last few months. It was so delicious that we forgot we were going to wake up in the morning wishing desperately that it wasn't Christmas morning — that we didn't have to get out of bed — talk — visit relatives all day long. Open presents? Oh no — too much energy. Be careful. Serves four.

2 cups Irish Cream
1/2 cup brandy
ice to top of blender

Put Irish Cream and brandy in blender. Fill to top with ice. Blend until very slushy. Serve immediately.

TRADITIONAL MEXICAN CHOCOLATE

(Non-Alcoholic)

True Mexican chocolate is sweet, hot and laced with cinnamon. It will please both kids and adults. It's perfect during cold weather when it's served the way the Latins like it — with hot, cinnamon-sugared churros (in the Dessert section). Makes 16 servings.

3 quarts milk
15 ounces semisweet chocolate squares
10 cinnamon sticks
1 tbsp vanilla

Combine milk, semisweet chocolate and cinnamon sticks in saucepan. Cook and stir just until chocolate melts. Remove from heat. Remove cinnamon and stir in vanilla. Beat with electric beater until frothy. Place cinnamon sticks into mugs and pour in hot chocolate. Serve immediately.

PUNTA MORRO STYLE MARTINIS

On the northern edge of Ensenada, hanging right out over the Pacific, is the exquisite gourmet restaurant, Punta Morro. It's the kind of place I reserve for celebrations marking special occasions. Nina and John, on the other hand, stop in for dinner nearly every time they're on their way to La Bufadora. It's that good! The presentation of their Martini is something right out of Hollywood. And the hint of Scotch they add to it makes it smooth, smooth, smooth! Just imagine your self sitting back, sipping your Martini as you watch those waves crash into the rocks below you and explode skyward. As the moonlight dances across the ocean's surface, check out the menu and order one of their mouth-watering dinners, served with home-grown vegetables from the nearby Guadalupe Valley. This recipe, shared with me by my waiter, serves two.

1 16 oz tin bucket (this looks like a tiny version of the standard old-fashioned bucket)
1 6 oz tin urn
1 1/2 cups ice and water

3 oz Gin or Vodka
3 splashes Vermouth
3 drops of Scotch
uo6 pimento-stuffed green olives
on toothpicks or plastic swords

Chill two Martini glasses in the refrigerator. Fill bucket with ice and water. In urn, mix Gin or Vodka with Vermouth and Scotch. Place in ice bucket to chill. Place a sword or toothpick with three skewered olives into each Martini glass. Serve the bucket of martinis with the two glasses and pour about an inch of liquor into each.

Hint: if you have no way of locating the bucket or urn — you can make these Martinis the old fashioned way in a shaker with slightly crushed ice. When thoroughly chilled, pour into Martini glasses and serve as above, leaving the shaker on the table so your guests can refill their own glasses.

DESSERTS

Full Moon Dancing

Desserts. You may not want to admit it, what with wasted calories and excess fat grams being so unpopular and all, but I bet this is your favorite section. It's mine! Well, maybe it's a tie with the salsas — and the — and the — oh, never mind!

I've included an array of desserts here from Baja and mainland Mexico, plus a few from the Caribbean, Spain, California and New Mexico. Many sound quite sophisticated, but I assure you, they aren't all that difficult to make.

Remember, we're not into slaving in the kitchen! We're into having a good time. We're into capturing some of that magic from south of the border and transporting it into your kitchen — and from your kitchen into your heart and your home.

Remember that. Remember to enjoy yourself — as you choose a dessert and get ready to prepare it tonight. If you find yourself forgetting what Baja Magic is, or even worse — forgetting what it feels like — open this book and allow yourself to be reminded.

One last thing. Remember? It's an attitude, it's an attitude, it's an attitude. It's an attitude most easily attained by changing the latitude, as Mr. Buffett has been reminding me for over 20 years. Think south. Think sky. Desert. Big, big blue ocean. Think pelicans. Whales. Margaritas. Street Tacos. Mariachis. Tequila. Friendly folks. Jimmy. Put on some music and get thyselves into the kitchen, amigos! Now give me an —

Ole!

Ole!

Ole!

MARC'S CITRUS FLAN EXTRAORDINAIRE

The day Nina and I met Marc Spahr at his Caffé Todos Santos, he sent this flan out to us as a gift after our meal. In all our years of traveling Baja and mainland Mexico, neither of us had ever, ever tasted flan this good. I consider it a real honor to have been entrusted with this recipe, and now it's yours too.

Marc was never formally trained as a chef. He came to Todos Santos, if you'll recall, to grow tropical fruits — and he's as successful a farmer as he is a restauranteur. Married now to a lawyer in La Paz, he's definitely integrated himself into the Southern Baja culture. He likes to tell the story of how he started cooking. His first attempts at baking were in a wood-fired brick oven on his farm. He started selling breads, cakes and cookies to the local gringo community. Pretty soon he was hired as head chef at the El Molino Restaurant in Todos Santos. By 1993 he'd taken the big step and opened his own restaurant.

If you ever are so fortunate as to find yourself in Todos Santos, make sure you stop in at Marc's restaurant. Try it for breakfast, lunch or dinner — or anytime in between. Sit in front in one of the hand-painted artsy chairs, or waltz through the kitchen (pure Baja-style) and eat outdoors in the cool, lovely patio. You won't be disappointed. No way José! Don't be surprised, either, if you run into Juan Carlos there! He goes absolutely crazy over this flan!

Coffee Caramel:
1/2 cup sugar
1/4 cup Expresso

Flan:
2 cups milk
1 cup heavy cream
1 cinnamon stick (4 inches long)
1 tbsp citrus zest (lemon, Mexican lime and/or orange)
1 tbsp pure vanilla extract
1/4 tsp nutmeg (fresh, grated)
1 cup sugar
6 egg yolks
3 eggs
1/8 tsp salt

Coffee Caramel:
In a small copper saucepan, mix sugar and coffee. Cook over medium heat, stirring only until sugar is dissolved. Then cook until syrup forms a soft ball when dropped into ice water. (If you have a candy thermometer, this happens at about 238° F) Pour mixture into mold — a nine-inch round, two-inch deep cake pan works well. Let the syrup set up in refrigerator while making flan.

Flan:
Preheat oven to 325°. In medium saucepan, combine milk, cream, vanilla, nutmeg, cinnamon stick and zests. Cook until almost boiling on

low heat, stirring, constantly. Pour mixture through fine sieve into a bowl. In another bowl, whisk together eggs, egg yolks, salt and sugar. Pour milk mixture slowly into egg mixture, whisking constantly.

Remove mold with caramel from refrigerator and pour flan into it. Set this mold inside a larger mold (a ten-inch round cake pan works) filled a quarter of the way up with water. Bake for one hour. Remove from oven and refrigerate for four hours.

To serve, loosen edges with a knife and invert onto a platter. Cut flan into eight wedges.

MARGARITA PIE

Margarita pie is a perfect way to end any elegant meal. Light, unusual and incredibly tasty, your guests will feel the essence of Baja Magic tickling their tongues as they slide that first bite of pie into their mouths. And they'll definitely be back for seconds. Serves eight.

1 package lemon pudding mix
1 package lime Jell-O mix
2 cups water

2 eggs, lightly beaten
1/3 cup lime juice
1/4 cup tequila
1/4 cup Mexican Controy, Cointreau or Triple Sec
1 1/2 cups whipped topping
1 9 inch graham cracker crust
1 lime, thinly sliced

Combine pudding mix and Jell-O mix. Stir in 1/2 cup water and beaten eggs. Blend well. Add remaining water and pour into medium sized sauce pan. Cook over medium high heat, stirring constantly until mixture comes to a full boil.

Remove from heat. Stir in lime juice, tequila and Controy and chill two hours. Fold whipped topping into chilled mixture. Spoon into pie crust and chill until firm, at least two hours. Garnish with lime slices.

CHURROS

Churros are Spanish doughnuts, squeezed out through a pastry bag and fried in long ribbons. In Spain they are served with piping hot chocolate. In the mall at La Bufadora, vendors wave them in front of your eyes, offering you a free sample in hopes that they can entice you to buy a bag for $1.00. You can also buy them as you wait in line to cross the border back into the U.S. Recipe makes 1 1/2 dozen churros.

1 cup water
1/4 tsp salt
1 tsp sugar
1/2 cup butter or margarine
1 cup flour
4 eggs
1/4 tsp lemon extract
1 cup corn or canola oil
1/2 cup sugar mixed with 1 tsp cinnamon

In a medium sized saucepan, combine water, salt, sugar and butter and bring to a full boil over high heat. Add flour and remove pan from heat. Beat mixture with spoon until smooth and it comes away from the sides of the pan. Add eggs, one at a time and beat well after adding each egg. Stir in lemon extract and cool for 15 minutes.

Put half the dough in a large pastry bag with a large star tip. Heat oil in deep skillet or deep fryer to 400 degrees. Squeeze dough into oil until you have a ribbon about 7 to 9 inches long. Cut it off with a knife. Fry 2 to 3 ribbons at a time for 6 or 7 minutes each. When golden brown, remove from oil and drain on paper towels.

Sprinkle with cinnamon sugar and serve warm.

SOPAPILLAS

Sopapillas have been a New Mexico favorite for hundreds of years. They made their way to Baja during the first half of this century. Derived from Indian fried bread, they are generally served hot with cinnamon and honey for dessert. Light and scrumptious! Makes approximately 20.

1 3/4 cups sifted flour
2 tsp baking powder
1/2 tsp salt
2 tbsp solid vegetable shortening
2/3 cup cold water
1 cup corn or canola oil
honey and/or cinnamon sugar to taste

Sift flour, baking powder and salt into a mixing bowl. Cut shortening in using two knives until it forms a coarse mixture. Gradually add cold water. Mix together just enough to hold together as you would if making a pie crust. Turn out on a lightly floured surface. Knead gently until smooth. Cover and let dough sit for five minutes. Roll into a rectangle about 12" x 15". Dough will be very thin.

Cut into rectangles about 2" x 3" in size. Heat oil until a drop of water sizzles when dropped into it in large skillet. Drop a few sopapillas at a time into the oil. Turn them over three to four times to make them puff up evenly, then fry for two to three minutes on each side, until they are golden brown and puffed up like small pillows. Dust with cinnamon sugar or pour small amount of honey over the sopapillas. Serve hot.

PINEAPPLE SOPAPILLAS

A delightful variation of sopapillas are these pineapple filled treats. By using the above recipe, and adding the filling you have a different dessert that will please adults and kids alike. Makes approximately 20.

Recipe preceding for sopapillas
(without cinnamon & honey)

2 1/2 tbsp granulated sugar
2 tbsp corn starch
1 1 lb 4 ounce can crushed pineapple, undrained (or any other canned fruit)
1/2 cup powdered sugar

Before frying the sopapillas, make the filling. In a medium sized

saucepan, combine granulated sugar and cornstarch. With wooden spoon, stir in pineapple. Cook mixture over medium heat, stirring constantly until boiling. Boil one minute, stirring and set aside to cool.

After sopapillas have been made, and while they are still hot, make a slit along one long side and one short side of each pillow with a sharp knife. Lift up the corner and fill each with a slightly rounded tablespoon of the filling. Sprinkle tops with powdered sugar and serve warm.

WATERMELON - LEMON ICE

Watermelon-lemon ice is an easy sherbet-like dessert that you can make with your kids' help. It's a refreshing after dinner treat during the hot months and one that will make you feel that you're barefoot under a palapa in San Felipe, La Paz or Los Cabos. Makes 1 1/2 pints.

2 cups pureed watermelon pulp
2 egg whites, stiffly beaten
1 6 ounce can frozen lemonade concentrate, thawed
3/4 cup water

Combine watermelon pulp, lemonade and water, Pour into freezing tray and freeze until mushy. Place in chilled bowl. Add egg whites and mix thoroughly. Return to tray and freeze until firm, stirring twice while freezing.

BAKED PINEAPPLE DELIGHT

Oh yum, yum, yum. Simple and exquisite, Baked Pineapple Delight combines the tastes of fresh fruit, rum and custard to create a memorable finale to any meal. Serves eight.

1 large or 2 medium sized pineapples
sugar to taste
3 tbsp rum
1/4 cup butter or margarine

Sauce:
2 cups half and half
1/4 tsp salt
1/4 cup sugar
1 egg
2 egg yolks
2 tsp corn starch
1 tsp vanilla

Lay pineapple on its side and take a thick slice from one side. Do not include green top. Set this slice aside. Carefully scoop out fruit and cut into bite-sized pieces.

Mix pineapple pieces with sugar to taste. Flavor with rum. Put pineapple pieces back into shell, dot with butter and cover entire pineapple with foil. Bake at 350 degrees for 20 minutes. While pineapple is baking, make sauce by stirring together half and half, salt, sugar, egg, egg yolks, cornstarch and vanilla. Cook over low heat, stirring constantly until smooth and slightly thickened. This will take about 10 minutes.

Chill until ready to serve. Serve pineapple warm with cold sauce on top and try not to blush when you get a standing ovation!

FRIED BANANAS MULEGE STYLE

Fried bananas were transplanted to Baja from Vera Cruz. Or Cozumel. Or some other exotic spot on the Gulf Of Mexico or in the Caribbean. I first tried these on my infamous trip to Mulege — that incredible tropical oasis almost two thirds of the way down the desert peninsula, that marks the

the desert peninsula, that marks the entrance to the equally incredible Bahía de Concepción. Both should go on your "to do" list for "must see" places. And this is a "must eat" dessert that my mom brought back with her that trip. Fried and lightly spiced with orange and cinnamon, it's a simple dessert that will please everyone.

In case you haven't heard much about Mulege, let me clue you in on a couple of things. First of all, it has the only navigable río in all of Baja. The river banks are lined with groves of date palms, coconut palms and olive trees. Mulege has a lovely mission, the incomparable and well-known Hotel Serenidad, and lots of offshore rock islands that colonies of sea lions call home. There are prehistoric cave paintings in the nearby hills — and of course — there's Bahía de Concepción. Aside from Los Arcos at Lands End in Cabo San Lucas, Mulege and Bahía de Concepción are undoubtably the two most-often photographed places in all of Baja. You just have to see them for yourself! This recipe serves eight.

4 tbsp butter or margarine
1/4 cup brown sugar
1/4 cup orange juice
1/2 tsp cinnamon

4 green tipped bananas, peeled and sliced lengthwise

Melt margarine in skillet with brown sugar, orange juice and cinnamon. Cook over medium heat until sugar dissolves. Add banana slices. Stir and cook over medium high heat for four to five minutes until bananas are golden and liquid is almost caramelized. Serve immediately.

BUÑUELOS

Buñuelos are sugared, fried tortillas. Popular and very easy to make, they're served all over Baja, mainland Mexico and the Southwest. (Taco Bell even has them these days!) Serves ten to twelve.

12 flour tortillas
1/2 cup corn oil
1 cup granulated sugar
1 tsp cinnamon
1/2 tsp ground cloves

Slice tortillas into eight wedges each. Heat oil in skillet over high heat until a drop of water sizzles when dropped into the pan. Fry tortilla wedges until crisp. Drain on paper towels.

On flat plate, mix sugar, cinnnamon and cloves. Coat tortilla wedges with sugar mixture. Serve warm or cool.

MAYAN MANGO MADNESS

From the deepest jungles of the Yucatán, where the Mayans once ruled, to the produce section at Calimax on the south end of Ensenada, you will never see mangos or papayas any bigger, sweeter or juicier than the ones they grow in Mexico. You can make this dessert with either mangos, papayas, strawberries or peaches. It's a truly delectable summer treat. Serves eight.

2 1/2 pounds fresh mangos, peeled and seeded or 1 20 ounce can mangos
(you can substitute papayas, strawberries or peaches)
1 cup water and 1/2 cup dissolved sugar or juice from the canned mangos
1 ounce brandy
3 3 ounce packages lady fingers
1 pint whipping cream
sugar to taste
1/2 tsp vanilla

1 cup pecans, 3/4 cup chopped only

Chop mangos into small pieces. Place fresh mangos in sugar and water, or return canned mangos to their syrup. Add brandy.

Dunk lady fingers into fruit syrup quickly one by one and line the bottom and sides of a 9 x 14 glass pan. Add a layer of chopped mangos.

Beat sugar, vanilla and whipping cream. Place a layer of cream and a layer of chopped pecans on top of the mangos. Alternate layers of lady fingers, mangos, cream and pecans, ending with whipped cream. Garnish with pecan halves.

Refrigerate three to four hours. Cut in squares to serve.

And enjoy.

Enjoy.

Enjoy.

INDEX

BEVERAGES, ALCOHOLIC

DESSERTS

Baked Pineapple Delight	203
Buñuelos	204
Churros	200
Fried Bananas Mulege Style	203
Marc's Citrus Flan Extraordinaire	198
Margarita Pie	200
Mayan Mango Madness	205
Pineapple Sopapillas	202
Sopapillas	201
Watermelon-Lemon Ice	202

ENCHILADAS

Carnitas Enchiladas	128
Chicken Enchiladas Suizas	121
Chicken Enchiladas Verdes	122
Chilequiles Vallarta	123
Crab Enchiladas Calafia Style	127
Stacked Cheese Enchiladas Taos Style	125

FAJITAS

Fajitas La Concha Beach Club Style	102
Grilled Fajitas Salad (with Chicken, Beef or Shrimp)	75

PORK

Carnitas Barbecues	101
Carnitas Enchiladas	128
Hot Carnitas Salad	74
Medallions of Pork Ixtapa Mulege Style	166
Rosarito Ribs de Fiero	161

POULTRY

Alta Cal's Caesar Salad with Chicken	75
Anita-Conchita's Chicken Mole	154
Caffé Todos Santos Chicken Flautas	33
Cataviña Chicken Rolls	151
Chicken Breasts with Santa Fe Chile Sauce	157

RELLENOS

RICE

SALADS

Marinated Vegetable Salad	64
Molded Gazpacho Salad	64
Spanish Rice Salad Santiago	60
Teaque Slaw	66
"The" Original Tijuana Caesar Salad	66
Watermelon Fruit Salad	65
Wilted Cabbage Salad	59

SALADS THAT MAKE A MEAL

Alta Cal's Caesar Salad (with Chicken, Beef or Shrimp)	77
Carne Asada Salad	75
Crab Salad Loreto	79
Ensalada Puerto de Illusion	78
Grilled Fajitas Salad (with Chicken, Beef or Shrimp)	75
Hot Carnitas Salad	74
Taco Salad	73
Wild West Barbecue Salad	80

SALSAS

In-a-Pinch Campsite Salsa	14
Marc's Mango Salsa Tropical	16
Salsa Chipotle	18
Salsa Fresca	13
Salsa Ranchera - Pancho Villa Style	15
Salsa Verde	16
Santa Fe Green Chile Salsa	17
Thick Sour Cream Sauce	19
Thin Sour Cream Sauce	19

SEAFOOD

Alta Cal's Caesar Salad with Shrimp	77
Avocado-Crab Cocktail	37
Batter Fried Shrimp Mazatlán Style	140
Bay of L.A. Lobster Tacos	116
Ceviche Gonzaga Bay Style	26
Chipotle Sea Bass with Vegetables	139
Crab Enchiladas Calafia Style	127

SOUPS

TACOS

Fish Tacos	114
Shredded Beef Tacos	109, 112
Chicken Tacos	109, 114
Turkey Tacos	109, 113
Rolled Tacos with Guacamole	32
Taco Salad	73

TOSTADAS
Beef Tostadas	111, 112
Chicken Tostadas	111, 113
Turkey Tostadas	111, 114
Los Arcos Ceviche Tostadas	117

TORTILLAS
Corn Tortillas	93
Flour Tortillas	93

VEGETABLES
Chef Carlos Leyva Valdez' Rajas en Crema	89
Chili Onion Rings	88
Papas Fritas con Chile Verde	84
Spa Vegetable Kabobs	86
Zucchini with Corn & Peppers	88

Restaurant Credits

Restaurant Pancho's in Cabo San Lucas
Salsa Ranchera - Pancho Villa Style
Caffé Todos Santos in Todos Santos
Marc's Mango Salsa Tropical
Caffé Todos Santos Chicken Flautas
Restaurante Palapa Azul at Tecolote Beach in La Paz
La Cola de la Sirena (Mermaid's Tail)
Restaurant Pancho's in Cabo San Lucas
Pancho's Tortilla Soup
Hotel Caesar's in Tijuana
"The" Original Caesar Salad
Celia's Restaurant in La Bufadora
Celia's Summer Nopales Salad
Buena Vista Beach Resort
Chef Carlos Leyva Valdez' Rajas en Crema
Las Conchas Beach Club in San Jose del Cabo
Fajitas Las Conchas Beach Club Style
Tío Pablos Restaurant in Los Barilles
Tío Pablo's Cabrilla Veracruzana
Restaurant La Bufadora in La Bufadora
Restaurant La Bufadora's Orphan Calamari
Restaurante Palapa Azula at Tecolote Beach in La Paz
Palapa Azul Stuffed Clams on the Grill
Los Gordos Restaurant in La Bufadora
Los Gordos Bloody Marys
El Dorado Restaurant in La Bufadora
El Dorado Mexican Coffee
La Concha Beach Resort in La Paz
Rumbas from the Palapa Bar
Punta Morro in Ensenada
Punta Morro Style Martinis
Caffé Todos Santos in Todos Santos
Marc's Citrus Flan Extraordinaire

Cooking with Baja Magic Order Form

Cooking with Baja Magic ($21.95 each)

Four easy ways to order:

1. Phone orders: (888) 736-6433 (Pacific Time)
2. Fax Orders: (619) 481-0947
3. E-mail: cookbaja@aol.com
4. Mail: Renegade Enterprises
        P.O. Box 1505
        Solana Beach, CA 92075

@ $21.95 #_____Cookbooks	$_____
(CA Only @ 7.75% Sales Tax	$_____
(Continental US) @ $3.95 per book Shipping &Handling	$_____
Sub-Total	$_____
Total	$_____

PAYMENT OPTIONS:

____Check or money order _____Master Card _____Visa _____American Express

Account # _____   Exp. Date _____

Signature _____

Enclosed is my check or money order for the amount of $ _____ payable to:
                                          RENEGADE ENTERPRISES

SEND TO:
Name: _____

Address _____

City/State/Zip _____

Daytime Phone _____

Please check here if you'd like to be added to our mailing list. ☐

Mi Casa Es Su Casa

Something Fishy

© Bob Bonn 1997

Love on the Ranch

© Bob Bonn 1997

Ann Hazard

The Author:

Ann Hazard is a third generation Baja Rat. She's been traveling the Magnificent Peninsula™ with her family, collecting recipes, since she was a child. She's flown into remote places in old World War II bombers and landed on dirt roads. She's camped on deserted beaches and in lush palm oases where her family was the only group of gringos for miles around. And of course, she's traveled to Los Cabos, La Paz, Loreto and all the hot spots the tourists frequent these days. A graduate of U.S. International University, Ann lives in Solana Beach, CA with her children, Gayle and Derek and an assortment of pets. She shares a weekend getaway with her sister, Nina and brother-in-law, John in La Bufadora — just a few miles south of Ensenada in Northern Baja. Her second book, Arise and Walk! will be out in 1998.

Bob Bonn

The Artist:

Bob Bonn's art grabs your senses and immediately transport you into a fantasy world of brilliant, pure color. His paintings are populated by grinning gatos (cats), laughing bulls, dancing cacti and a wonderful collection of other Wild West Baja characters. The son of a well-known Laguna Beach artist, Bob was raised with a solid appreciation for technique and color. Educated at Cal State Northridge and U.C. Santa Barbara in drawing and fine art, Bob created and refined his own style over the years. His ability to select an image and infuse it with bold design elements and raw color has given his presentations an original, dramatic flair. It has also brought him considerable success in Southern California. Bob resides in Laguna Beach with his wife Maria and cat, Batman.